MARK SALOMON

SIMPLICITY

[RELEVANTBOOKS]

Published by Relevant Books
A division of Relevant Media Group, Inc.

www.relevant-books.com
www.relevantmediagroup.com

Cover Design by Tony Streeter, Jeremy Kennedy
Interior Design by Jeremy Kennedy, Tony Streeter
www.relevantsolutions.com

International Standard Book Number: 0-9760357-6-6

This book was previously published in 2003 by Skeleton Key Publishing:
www.skeletonkeypublishing.com.

For information or bulk orders:
RELEVANT MEDIA GROUP, INC.
100 South Lake Destiny Drive Suite 200
Orlando, FL 32810
PH: (321) 206-8844

05 06 07 08 9 8 7 6 5 4 3 2 1

Printed in the United States of America

ACKNOWLEDGMENTS

I have to say thanks to a few people here who have made writing this not only possible, but also worthwhile ...

To Stephanie, who helped me keep my focus and desire on this beast, thank you. (The hammer and chisel, removing the big pieces ...)

To Deanne Neubauer. Without her patient editing skills, you probably wouldn't have come this far without throwing the whole tangle of thoughts into a toilet. I can't thank her enough for her help. (Basically, double-bass pedals are the pretty much the coolest things when you kind of sort of need that stuff.) YOU ROCK!

Steve Fosmire is the reason that this book is not on newsprint ... or, for that matter, still on the hard drive of my iBook.

Peter Melby of Netfire Designs was an amazing help and has been for a long time, from running the Stavesacre and Skeleton Key Publishing sites to taking pictures in the wee hours of the morning. Thank you very much.

I'd also like to thank Joe Cuello for his early perspective and assistance. He's the reason that some of these stories make sense. ("Oh, yeah ... you don't know what I'm talking about, do you?") Maybe we can get that introduction later, when you're not making an amazing film (The Last Words of Gustavo and Maria Cuello).

Special thanks to Bill Power and the guys of MxPx, for turning me onto a great book, Addicted to Mediocrity, by Franky Schaeffer. It had a lot to do with this one, but was better written. (Hard to believe, I know ... but it's true.)

My sister Lora and my brother Jason, and my families—Brownells and Cookseys.

Oh yeah, and my parents ... if you still want me to be your kid after all of this.

A special thanks also goes to the long lost photographers: Bonnie Lee Groth and Perry Cooper. Perry shot many press photos for the Crucified, and Bonnie always seemed to be floating around the stages at Cornerstone. A special thanks to Tammy and Lawanda, who came back from Never-Never Land with a lot of new photos for this edition. The other ones were, of course, shot by me mum.

The families and friends who helped put Humpty back together again—sometimes at 3 a.m.: Robert and Edie Goodwin. Julia Griffin. Kevin and Tanya Kribs. Freddie and Mary Jo Piro. Dan and Stacie Richard. Dan and Shauna Snow.

I would like to also thank these people for either inspiring, influencing, or encouraging: all the bands, businesses, and groups that the Crucified and Stavesacre have had the blessing of being involved with. Any member, past, present, consistent, or sporadic of the Saint John Backyard Firepit Philosophers. Tim Anderson. David Bahnsen. Jay Bakker. Balmers. Jeff Bellew. David Bianco. Blindside. The Bookman Too in Huntington Beach. Aaron Bradford★. Derrick, Sarah, and Keith Callegari. Bryan Carlstrom. Chaffins. Eric Churchill★. Rodney Clark. Jeff Cloud. Scott Cochran (and Mia and Java Jungle). Eric and Carla Collins. Paul Cruikshank (and Ragin' Records R.I.P.). Linda Davis. Denison Marrs. Darin Dennee. Lisa Donini. Pigeon John Dunkin. Brandon Ebel and Tooth & Nail Records. Adam Ferry. Jessica Fife. Fresno People. Echocast. Embodyment. Adam Ferry. Ghoti Hook (R.I.P.). Rudy Gonzales. Jessica Holmes. Jeff Holmes. Huntington Beach People. Initium Eyewear. Jesus People USA. Stephen King. Kevin, Tanya, Tori, and Kati Kribs. Mark and Mary Lemmenes. C.S. Lewis. Mike Lewis. Madera People. Tim Mann. MxPx (with J.J. Janes very much in mind). Marvel Comics. Minor Threat. Nitro Records. Gary Nixon. Larry Norman. The O.C. Super-tones. Outer Circle. Bill Power. Project 86. P.O.D. Puller (R.I.P.). Vanessa Righton (Ebel). Scandinavian People. Scaterd Few. Sid's Tattoo. Jimmy and Renée Steele. Kris and Laura Stencel. J.R.R. Tolkien. U2. Vans Warped Tour. David "Burrito" Villapando and Sparky's Barbershop/Red Dragon Tattoo (that's his Crucified tattoo by the way ... 8-Ball Cholos por Vida). Matt Wignall. Xs Records.

To my attorney, Lisa Donini, thanks—nice to have The Queen on my side.

I obviously have to thank Stavesacre and the Crucified for shaping my life ... the Crucified was a blur, but something that still impacts me and a lot of other people today. Stavesacre is still my favorite band and still my favorite group of people to be around. I love rock and roll. We'll see what comes next ... Sovereignty is a two-edged sword.

I hope.

—M

FOREWORD

The author of this book has a rare distinction. He is one of the only men in the world (aside from my father and a few drill sergeants) who has made me cry on more than one occasion.

I guess I should explain.

I've known Mark Salomon since we were teenagers in the early 1980s. He was the singer in a group called The Crucified, and I was the singer/bassist in a San Diego band that had recently changed our name from Pontius Pilate & The Pious Punks to Point Blank for reasons that should be pretty obvious.

Around 1985 we hit the road to play our first out-of-town gig in Fresno, California. Mark had invited us to play with his band at a local church. During the course of the weekend, my bandmates and I were the recipients of free pizza, free ice cream, and a full spread breakfast courtesy of Mark's mom. I can still remember waking up on the couch with the smell of home cooking flowing into my nostrils. I thought to myself, "WOW! Being in a band is the greatest scam ever! People pay you to play music, give you a place to sleep, and everywhere you go, they feed you for free!"

About a decade and four or five bands later ... when I was on tour and the show sucked, or we got ripped off, or there was no place to sleep and we had to drive all night (insert one of the many horrors of being a working class musician here), I would secretly curse Fresno and that d--- breakfast. I know it's not his fault, but to this day, I still joke that he should have warned me that things were going to get ugly.

Fast forward to 1999. In the years between, I had been married and divorced, not of my choosing. The Cruci-fied had called it quits, and Mark had a new group called Stavesacre. One day while talking on the phone, Mark told me that a song called "Gold & Silver" on Stavesacre's latest album was partially inspired by my experience. After we got off the phone I popped in the CD and read the lyrics while Mark sang: *And I know where you're going ... And that's the hardest part .... No matter where tonight ends ... You won't escape your broken heart.*

I broke down and wept.

Later that summer, I sat on the side of the stage as Staves-acre performed at a festival to a supercharged audience. They played the song, and for the duration of it, I cried like I have never cried. I felt a weight in my heart was lifting. At the crescendo of the song, I sang along as loud as I could manage, Under wings of gold and silver ... Sometimes we have to hide ... For shelter from this bitter winter ... At least tonight ... stay a while.

I thank God for Mark. I don't know if I've ever told him.

As I read this book for the first time, I was astonished by it. I burned through the pages as if my life depended on getting to the end. I felt like in a lot of ways, his story was mine as well. And maybe, like me, you'll find a little bit of yourself in here, too.

While this volume is serious in many ways, it is also very

funny. Maybe I just have a dark sense of humor, but I found myself laughing aloud as I read many of the stories. You know when you have a day or week (or a life) that is so bad that when the next disaster strikes, all you can do is laugh like a maniac? It's sort of like that.

I'm not sure if my friend was trying to be ironic with the title Simplicity. I've known the man for nearly twenty years, and "simple" is not a word that comes to mind when I think about him or his life. But don't take my word for it. Read on and decide for yourself.

Stay a while ... There's so much more to tell.

Bill R. Power
La Mirada, California, June 2003

CONTENTS

STAVESACRE today— (Neil Samoy, Ryan Dennee, Sam West, Mark Salomon, Dirk Lemmenes)

INTRODUCTION

Your smile looks like a grimace

On the fifth week of a seven-week tour, my band, Staves-acre, pulled into the back alley of a church in Washington state, preparing for yet another show in what had been a steady stream of many weeks of fake smiles, small talk, and uncomfortable exchanges. Every night there was a new church, another "Christian event," or something called an "outreach" where we would show up and try our best to put on a happy face, supposedly reminding ourselves that this was "worth it if it paid the bills." During those weeks, we told anyone and everyone who would listen that despite whatever expectations they might have, we weren't a min-istry or an evangelistic band, but that we were entertainers in the entertainment business. We didn't want to be held to the assumed role of "ministry tool" or to be perceived as a vehicle in some complete stranger's outreach plans—we were a band that got paid to play our music and show people a good time.

The album we were touring to support, *Speakeasy*, our third full length, was an album full of songs about changing our situation and finding one that we could exist in with some peace of mind. At this point, we still felt justified in complaining about all the things we were going through. It didn't feel like complaining back then; it felt like thinking out loud. We felt persecuted, judged, and perceived as villains, and night after night, we quietly cursed our situation. The daily defense of our position, and the daily defense of our relationships with God, had been going on for the five or six years we had been touring churches and doing Christian shows. We rarely met up with people who we felt immediate fellowship with; in fact, most of the time, we felt a complete absence of it. If we weren't questioned—by what we came to recognize as the "Christian Inquisition"— about our own spirituality, we were questioned about the spirituality of friends of ours. Much of the time we spent talking to the fans at the shows, or even the promoters, it was often apparent that we weren't really defending our relationships with God as something that we might or might not have, but as something we most likely didn't have at all, or worse—had forsaken. After a while, we got to the point where we just didn't want to talk to anyone anymore, and if we could pull it off, we probably would have been just fine with loading in our gear and playing our show without having to speak to a single person outside of the band.

What we really were was a group of bitter guys who had done this dance for too long and needed to make a change as soon as possible. In the back of our minds was the reality that we were the ones who signed off on the shows we played, and continued to allow ourselves to be booked into these same kinds of situations. (This was something easy to forget with the always-comforting knowledge that we could play music for a living when we were on tour, and we always made payroll.)

At the very end of the previous tour, "Vanna" (our much maligned van) threw a rod and was banished to a repair shop high in the Colorado Rockies, where it would remain for almost a year. For this tour, we had to find alternate modes of transportation. For the first three weeks, we rented an ancient RV, and for the remaining four, a Penske moving truck. (The RV was christened "Irv," and the Penske was known very imaginatively as "The Truck" or "The Penske." Aren't we clever?)

Irv had been an adventure. It was the size of a bus, with the suspension of a broken-down jalopy one might see rotting in a field somewhere in Nebraska. The driver's side front end leaned down and to the left, while the other three corners of the motor home remained somewhat suspended in their rightful positions. When the wind blew, which was constantly while on the road in places like Texas or Oklahoma, the motor home blew all over the place, rocking back and forth and nearly sweeping the other cars off of whatever freeway we were on. When we finally switched out of Irv for The Truck, we considered ourselves the luckiest band in the world.

The Truck was your standard Penske moving truck, temporarily converted the way most bands would convert them ...

A medium sized Penske moving van is set up in two parts: the cab and the cargo area. The cargo area housed the gear, a couple futons, a couch, and two or three people. The cab would of course hold the driver and one passenger. By opening the small sliding door between the two front seats in the cab, those in the cargo area kept their connection to the outside world—and the air conditioning.

We put the futons toward the front of the cargo area. This way, if you were laying on the futons with your head toward the front of the truck while the sliding door was open, you could carry on a conversation with the driver and whoever was sitting shotgun. (But you would also be blocking the a/c—so don't do that.) We plugged our cigarette lighter power converter into the dashboard and then attached a six-foot long power strip to it, which we ran through the sliding door and back into the cargo area. There we set up our television and Playstation 2 (mandatory tour equipment) next to the futons. Ideally, two people would be riding up front, while the rest of the band lounged in the cargo area. Behind the two futons, at about the halfway point of the cargo area, we put a small couch, which performed two functions: It gave anyone who wanted it a proper seat and also provided a somewhat firm place to stack gear. The gear would be stacked between the back of the couch and the big roll-up cargo door, taking up the back half of the cargo area. If you were to open the roll-up cargo door at the back of the truck for loading or unloading gear while someone was sitting on the couch playing video games, you could only see the backs of their heads, just above the gear and the back of the couch. Got it?

After getting this image clear in your head, you might ask: How safe is that?

The answer to that question is: Not very. Nothing was nailed down.

With only futons—without frames—and bodies supporting the distance between the couch and the front of the cargo area, any time we had to stop quickly or—God forbid—slam on the brakes, everything slid forward. Nothing was nailed down, not the couch or the gear or anything. This predicament became known as "The Taco" or "Tacoing," and it was terrifying. For instance, some of us might be in the back, sleeping to the gentle hum of the truck in the darkness of the cargo area's lightless box. Should the person driving have to slam on the brakes to keep from hitting Bambi, whoever was in the back would wake to find their bodies wrapped up in futons and other bodies, with a couch and a couple guitar cabinets looming overhead. You could feel everything just wanting to come forward whenever The Truck stopped, but you didn't want to think of what would happen should we have to stop dead while going sixty or seventy miles an hour.

It was just such a predicament that we found ourselves in that day we rolled into the alley. We had been on the road all night and most of the day, with traffic, winding roads, and the ever-present dread of the coming evening's Christian Show, so tensions were high. Dirk, our bass player, was driving, and Ryan (guitar) was in front. I was in the back with Neil (more guitars) and Sam (drums). Something I forgot to mention was that during the day, the cargo area was also very much like a green house, with the roof being nothing more than an opaque plastic covering—when the sun was shining, it was light enough in the cargo area to read, but also very hot. This, along with the dust that seems to come as a standard feature in moving trucks, did not help our overall attitude.

We were almost to the venue—which was a good thing because we all had to go to the bathroom—when Dirk had to hit the brakes suddenly. Taco Time. Everything squished forward, including the futon I was laying on, and it startled me. I had already been in a bad mood, which was not unusual on tours such as this one, and when we tacoed, I snapped at Dirk to be careful. Dirk, who was being no less careful than he always was, didn't appreciate my little comment, which came from the cargo area and probably seemed a bit more forceful than was at all necessary.

Dirk and I grumbled at each other as we pulled into the alley. We parked by the load-in door at the back of the church, and Dirk, in his usual, even tone, said my rebuke was a little silly, especially coming from me—the guy who flips out whenever anyone, in any way, is critical of his driving. This was a humbling thing to hear, which, along with my bad attitude, added a little self-defensiveness on my part to the whole situation. We talked it out, and got out of The Truck to help the guys load in our gear. Even with our mini-make-up session, feelings were still hurt, and the general mood was ... sour.

As we got out, a man was standing in the alley doorway of the church. He was big, probably around six-two, and on the stocky side. His arms were folded, and he was just sort of standing, staring off into the distance above the buildings that lined the alley. I remember the day as being sunny and bright, which was a pretty rare thing for the state of Washington. I looked up around the buildings to see what he was looking at, which turned out to be nothing. I gave a token greeting to the guy, who then gave me a token response, and I walked past him into the church.

I still had to go to the bathroom pretty bad. We had played at this church once before, and I remembered where the restrooms were, so I made my way down the stairs, past the little café they had in the lower level of the building, and into the restroom. Then something horrible happened: While using the urinal in the bathroom, I pissed all over the front of my pants. I freaked out. I was tired, hot, upset, and embarrassed at the way I had treated Dirk earlier ... and I now had urine all over the front of my pants. Break it down any way you want to, and no matter what person you might be talking about, no one wants to be seen with a big circle of darkness around their fly. For me it might have been just a little more foul, because I am the biggest freak about cleanliness, and sterile or not—urine is still urine.

As inconspicuously as I could, I made my way back to the alley door of the church where I incorrectly assumed that The Truck still sat parked. As far as I could tell, no one noticed me, so I thought I might have a chance to get into some clean clothes before people started showing up for the gig. Not only was I incorrect in assuming The Truck was still where it had been when we parked, I also didn't escape everyone. I popped out the back door to find The Truck gone and the big guy, the one who had been standing in the doorway when we got there, now standing where The Truck had been.

I tried to do a kind of spin-move, attempting to turn around and head back into the cover of the venue until I could find an alternate route to wherever The Truck now was, but I failed miserably. By trying my fancy little move and attempting to shield my new, round, wet stain from the big guy's view, I mostly just stood in one place in the alley, wiggling around like a bad dancer. I was looking at the guy's eyes, to see if he was looking down at my pants, when he looked me dead in the eye and immediately started talking to me.

Oh no.

The big guy wasn't just any big guy; he was the pastor of the church. He asked me if I was ready to "have the Gospel go out tonight," and if I was going to be of assistance in that process or a hindrance to it. I told him that we would be more than willing to let him do his thing at his church. I then told him that we weren't going to preach because that wasn't really the kind of band we were, and that we didn't go about things in that way, etc.

Then, he smiled. Kind of. He looked like he was wincing, as if he had just stubbed his toe. It seemed like he was trying to say something with that smile ... I just didn't know how to respond to it, so I blew it off.

He continued on, "The Gospel will go out tonight. You can believe it. I am the pastor of this church, and one way or another, the Gospel will go out tonight." I was having trouble keeping up with the conversation, because I was still thinking about the argument Dirk and I had earlier, about how I wanted to get to where he was so I could be sure everything was all right ... and about the front of my pants. After a while, my mind focused on the conversation, and I realized he might be implying that we'd possibly do something to prevent the Gospel from "going out," which I thought was odd. I could feel myself getting irritated, and I felt a little harassed, but I tried to keep my cool.

He kept repeating himself, and I kept standing there, trying not to let the urine stain show and trying not to respond with anything that could be construed as offensive or defensive. Every time he said the thing about the Gospel, he punctuated it with one of those wincing smiles. Feeling a little panicked now about the stain situation and slowly realizing someone who expected an audience had cornered me, I stated once again that I had no problem with him speaking at his church. I told him that there were a lot of reasons why we didn't preach from the stage, and that we felt much more comfortable in places like our jobs and our regular hangouts when it came to sharing our faith—places where we could build relationships and maintain them. I talked about my job at the time, a coffee shop back home in Huntington Beach, and about the relationships I had been able to build there, that that was my mission field. I didn't mention that I didn't understand why he would charge money for the Gospel—disguised as a rock show or not—it was his place, and I wasn't going to get in the way of what he called his "vision." What he did with the church God had put in his care was between him and God. I kept nodding "yes" while maintaining that we weren't going to change our beliefs simply because he wanted us to. I couldn't cut things off just to change my pants either, because I felt like we needed to come to some sort of understanding. One way or another, this guy was going to arrive at his own conclusion—that much was clear—and I was going to do my best to influence that conclusion in a positive way.

The conversation ended with him walking away and

looking over his shoulder saying, "The Gospel will go out tonight."

I replied, "Okay," and went to find The Truck and some clean clothes.

———————————— ✦ ————————————

We were in the backstage area right before the show started, and there had apparently been some words between the pastor and one of the bands we were playing with, as well as with one of our guys. Everyone was a little on edge and feeling very unwelcome. You could hear guys talking about "that weird pastor-guy" while they were getting ready to play.

When we finally played our set, I said something to the effect that I wasn't much of a pastor, that I would obey God rather than men whenever I could, and that for some people, that was just not going to be enough. I shouldn't have said anything, because I was upset, and there was no way I was going to say anything completely positive—but I really wanted to shut the guy up, and at that point of the tour, I was sick and tired of walking on eggshells with people like him. Not a good time to have a microphone. I let the crowd know that we just wanted to give them their money's worth of music, and call it a night. Truthfully, the kids seemed to appreciate it. We played our set and tried to enjoy ourselves.

After we were done playing, the pastor came on stage and made a long speech. He began by preaching what seemed to have been his original message, but he closed it with a few offhanded comments about an ambiguous group of people who might be ashamed of the Gospel. It was uncomfortable, and the people in the audience just looked at him and tried to figure out what he was talking about.

The pastor met us on the way to The Truck. There was a lot of staring and glaring. When he paid us, he said that we "got what we came for" and now we could go.

It was weird. We got out of there as quickly as we could, and I remember thinking I was glad the whole experience was over.

Once again, I was incorrect ...

———————————— ✦ ————————————

Java Jungle is a coffee shop in downtown Huntington Beach—also known as "H.B."—and to me it embodies the spirit of the town itself. It's right on the corner of 6th Street and Pacific Coast Highway, across from the beach, and is the longest standing—and to most of its regular customers, only—coffee shop in the area.

When I first moved to Huntington in '93, all of my friends told me not to go to "Java" at night—there was too much drama, a lot of drugs, a lot of fights, and generally a lot of trouble. The young and wild crowd tend to hang around Java Jungle just for kicks, but also because it's about the closest thing to a community fixture that a lot of the younger people in Huntington have known. It's open from 4:30 a.m. to 2 a.m. on the weekdays, and until 3 a.m. on the weekends so underage people can go there to hang out and catch up on what's what, then meet up with their drinking aged friends when the bars close. Because it's such a hang out and yet not a bar or a club, there are also a lot of people involved in Alcoholics and Narcotics Anonymous mixed in as well. At the shop, just like in the town, there is always something going on. I worked there for about five years, and still frequent the place to this day.

Some very interesting characters from all walks of life come through Java Jungle. Early on, there were a lot of neo-Nazis and people with "WHITE POWER" tattooed on the backs of their arms, their stomachs, their necks ... their foreheads. Even after cleaning up the image of the place from those days, there are still a lot of ex-cons and guys

with unsettling tattoos on their bodies or intimidating looks
on their faces who hang around and are regular customers.
(Strangely enough, a lot of Orange County is just like that.
It's normal. Very odd to a person originally from central
California's San Joaquin Valley, a fairly ethnically diverse
place where that sort of thing is decidedly not normal and
likely to cause a riot.)

Huntington, like most beach communities, is full of every
kind of person you can imagine—from homeless people
who shadowbox the air, to local trippers who somehow
make a living by selling bike parts and jewelry, to super-
rich yuppies who live in million-dollar homes right off of
the beach. There are the typical surfer types of course, but
they're only a fraction of the kinds of people who make up
most southern California beach towns. I've seen a guy waving knives in the air at imaginary beings, while only a few
yards away, a couple of young ladies studied for their winter
semester finals—and both of them were sitting at the tables
right out in front of the coffee shop. I have met homeless people who are nice and ones who are very much not
nice. There are jumpy cops everywhere. For every woman
with completely natural features, there's one with ... various
enhancements.

The list goes on an on—the point is: The town and the
shop alike see all kinds. Nevertheless, it's the town I live
in, and among these people, I have found a place where in
spite of all my failures, God somehow uses me to be a light
in a dark place.

———————————— ✿ ————————————

I believe God has given me a unique opportunity there,
one that continues even now that I don't really work there
anymore. The people I used to serve were regulars long
before I came around and were mostly a private crowd. A
lot of them have reason to be—there is something about

a community of people closely associated with prison that tends to lean toward the very private. (Java has been nicknamed "the Yard" since it was built—with so many of our regulars having some kind of penal history that it has often resembled a prison yard—just without all the weights and matching jumpsuits.) When I first started working there, none of the regulars would talk to me—I was new, and they didn't know anything about me. After getting to know me, I was mostly embraced with open arms, sometimes as "the Christian" and sometimes as just a nice guy. Eventually, I earned the trust of a lot of my customers. There have been a few precious instances when someone going through difficult times felt comfortable coming to me about what was going on, knowing I would respect their privacy and pray for them. There have been moments when I could see that God had given me the opportunity to be a missionary to the speed freaks, strippers, ex-cons, and general knuckleheads of the community—and I feel blessed for it.

I will never be a "Huntington Beach Native," but I make my home there, and the people of the town—many of whom I've met at Java Jungle—have made me feel like part of the community. I believe that this pleases God. You see, in our town, there are people who come down to the main hangouts—but never Java Jungle, strangely—on Friday nights, from cities far away from Huntington, to "reach out to all the lost souls" of our "haven of sin." They feel a "special burden" for the people of my town—at least the ones on Main Street, where the sidewalks are packed all night long on the weekends—and so they come, dozens of them from twenty miles away, with flyers, bullhorns, tracts, and big signs that say things like, "Repent for the Kingdom of God is Near." They pass these tracts out and have heated discussions with drunken people and partiers about their souls, while the merchants of every store on Main Street just hope that not all of their walk-up business will be scared away. They come and they go. Meanwhile, the "lost souls" remain in Huntington, many of whom will remember the people with the bullhorns and the tracts mostly because they have to clean up after them the next day, when the ticker-tract parade has come and gone again.

There is a lot of bitterness in my town, and a lot of it has to do with this strange representation of Christianity. God has blessed me with a great opportunity to be different from the weirdoes who come with all of their yelling and grandstanding about heaven and hell, only to leave again until the next "Outreach Night" gets planned.

There are people who need help, and they know they need help, and there are those who don't feel in need of any help at all. I have built relationships with both—not because I meant to, like some kind of experiment or something, but because I worked there at the shop, and, through time, I got to know all kinds of people. I have been around them on my good days and my bad ones, and they see and know that I don't think I'm any better than they are. This, to me, is at least the beginning of true religion: being yourself, and being a friend. It takes time, doesn't provide the immediate results many Christians favor, and requires a lot more humility than one might start off with. Some Christians (I think often because of temptations that they might deal with on their own) can't see how a person could be a friend to some of the people I've been blessed to know without joining in the lifestyles they lead. I don't really have time for that sort of thought though, or for trying to prove those people wrong. I would rather just live and be available—let whoever think whatever they want. I have found that regardless of what anyone might think, I have built good relationships with a lot of my regulars at the Jungle, in the same way I've built relationships at any of the jobs I've held—and God has reflected off of me in that setting, sometimes in the strangest ways ...

The owner of Java has essentially left the door open for me to have a job there if I need one. Because of that, after the "Seven Week Tour of Death," I sat behind the counter taking care of business once again, with The Truck and Irv far behind me.

One afternoon, a couple of my regulars were at the shop visiting me, along with the usual nameless/faceless customers, when from out of nowhere, kids started pouring in through the front door. Some of them were wearing T-shirts with Christian band names and slogans on them, and they were staring at me and whispering to each other. I saw a couple kids point at me and head to the counter. I thought to myself: "What's this all about?"

One of them came up to the counter, and soon three or four of his friends were standing behind him. He ordered a drink and then asked me if I was the singer of Stavesacre. I told him that I was, and as soon I responded and we began to have a conversation, all of the kids jumped in as well. I found out that they were from that same church venue up in Washington State, and had been at the show the night we played. They said they had a great time at the show, that they liked our music, and were curious about when we would be coming back up to play. They were actually really cool, and I didn't want to say the wrong thing—it was obvious that they were just fans who had no idea about what had happened backstage at the show. I told them we would probably be up in the area soon enough, that they should keep their eyes on the tour dates posted on our website, and that it would be great to see them at the next show. They skipped right past my generic response and then asked when we would be back at their church. They weren't all that interested in our tour plans; they wanted us to come back to their place. This kept on for a minute or two, and

I eventually had to tell them we probably wouldn't play at their church again, and that we didn't think their pastor would want to bring us back up anyway.

They were disappointed to hear this, and maybe even a little surprised. They said things like, "Hey! No way! Why wouldn't he like you guys? That show was a lot of fun." They told me they listened to our album all the time, that in fact they'd just been listening to it on their way down to California.

Something was weird from the beginning of the conversation, and I couldn't put my finger on it at first ... then everything became clear. As they were saying these things, their pastor walked through the front door.

Ahhh. I get it.

At first, I didn't really grasp why they were in southern California. They told me they were on their way to a mission trip in Mexico, and now it was clear that their pastor had planned to make a little stop along the way. Was it coincidence that they stopped in Huntington Beach, of all the places they could have stopped, and that they also just so happened to stop by Java Jungle? Or were they here in response to what I had told their pastor about my job down in Huntington where I felt that God had given me an opportunity to be a witness? Was this guy still ticked off about us not doing what he wanted us to do at his show? So upset that he was determined to come down to my town and make me prove that my so-called mission field wasn't a sham? As the reality of what was going on became clearer and clearer, I got more and more upset. I knew the kids probably didn't have anything to do with this, but I could only fear what this man had told them they were here to do.

The pastor walked up to the counter, ordered a drink, and sat down. I decided not to let my temper get the best of me—something that was well on its way to happening— and just tried to be nice. I asked how things were going and made some small talk. He sat at the counter and didn't say much at all. A friend of his, another adult, who by the way he carried himself looked like he might be in some kind of leadership role with the group, came in. He leaned on one of the chairs that sat around a table in the middle of the shop and didn't say anything. At that point I started feeling ambushed. I was at work and couldn't leave. I was cornered again, and knowing what he had been like up in Washington, I had all new fears as to what he would be like here.

I served him his drink, made the small talk, and then went back to work, taking care of another customer who had come in behind him.

As I served the other customer his drink, the pastor asked, "So ... where's your attitude?"

I tried not to show my surprise. "My attitude?" I asked. "What attitude? I'm working; this is just how I am while I'm here."

"Your attitude. The one you brought to my church and infected my youth with?"

And then it came: the wincing smile.

I had no idea where to start.

My attitude? Keep this up, and you'll find it easily enough.

I was suddenly very aware of my surroundings. I was aware of the factthat I was in Java Jungle. I was aware of the kids who had come in first, who were now sitting around the shop, staring in quiet confusion at their pastor and me. I was aware of a couple of my regulars who had come to visit me but were now looking very uncomfortable. All other conversation in the shop had completely stopped, and now the pastor and I were on center stage.

The conversation picked up. Right then I decided that I wanted to know exactly what this was all about, that if this guy was intent on coming in to my job, around a group of people I was trying to be a friend to—in contrast to people just like him—to prove some kind of point, I wanted that point on the table, immediately.

"I'm not sure why you're here while I'm working, but if you came in to argue with me or try to make me look bad, I really don't appreciate it. I didn't have any more of an attitude with you than the one you had with all of us when we were at your church."

He replied, "You came into my church with your bad attitude, infected the young people that I watch over there with that attitude, got paid, and then left. I paid you ____ dollars, and for what? You wouldn't even give a simple message."

From there, the conversation got more heated and intense very quickly.

He told the kids from his youth group to go to the "Christian Coffeehouse" down the street and around the corner. He then started in on how much we were paid again, and how much we wouldn't comply with all of the things he expected from us. I was instantly furious. I told him that if he had a problem with the kind of money we made, he shouldn't have brought us up in the first place, and that it wasn't fair for him to additionally hold that against us because we didn't see things the way he did. The basic thrust of what was bothering this pastor was that we were paid some amount of money that he felt should have justified his demands regarding what we did onstage, and that we had ultimately stolen from him and his church because we got paid this amount of money and didn't preach. He said I had a bad attitude from the moment I got to his church, from our first conversation in the alley, and that the entire time I was there I had shown him nothing to prove otherwise.

Now where could I go? I told him that he had no idea what had transpired before we got to his place, and that he was mistaken regarding my attitude during the conversa-

tion we had in the alley. I had to go through the process of
explaining to him the argument I had with Dirk, the rough
tour, and the urine incident. Nothing. He couldn't care less.
He just kept on.

I told him that we never claimed to be a ministry, and
that it seemed kind of unfair of him to imply that we had
misrepresented ourselves and then hold the amount of
money we were paid against us like some kind of proof of
whatever. All of this from behind the counter of one of the
few places on earth where I felt like I had been successful
in living out the Gospel message in my life. All of this while
my friends and regulars sat around and stared in total
confusion.

All of this with that grimace of a smile. He punctuated
everything he said with it.

I started to raise my voice, because I was getting frustrated
and the conversation was going nowhere. I felt like the guy
had a bone to pick, and that he wasn't going to leave until
he felt like he had won some kind of victory. I asked him
who he thought he was, coming in to my job over a month
after the show to hash this out. He had the contact information for the booking agent we were using at the time.
He could have called them, and if all of this was so upset-
ting to him, he could have gotten a hold of me some way,
and we could have talked it out like gentlemen. We could
have reasoned and worked out whatever was going to get
worked out. Instead, he let the situation sit until he could
come into my job and have it out with me.

I felt like he had something to prove, like he was coming into my job—the one I had told him about when
explaining our position on preaching at shows, attempting
to describe to him a place I felt real ministry was possible
in my life—with the purpose of "putting me in my place,"
which seemed a lot less like ministry and a lot more like his
own pride. I was also getting more and more upset about

the fact that by forcing his hand here of all places, the work that I been doing was unraveling right in front of me: more Christians who were creepy, more Christians arguing—not that I thought he had anything to complain about. I maintained that if his expectations regarding the "ministry" aspect of the show were unclear, he should have defined them. I told him I was sorry if he was misinformed, and that if he had intended to have a group delivering a sermon, then he should have booked one that did—we have made our position as clear as we could, from our official contracts to our interviews. As much as we could do, we had done. (Or at least, as much as we could have done and still played those shows ... but more on that later.) When he booked the show, he had an agenda we didn't agree with or conform to, so in response, he threw a fit.

His understanding of what a band's function should be was completely different than mine, and he had come to my job to set me straight.

My emotions got the best of me. I tried to keep them under control, but the guy just wouldn't stop. He kept repeating the same things. He wasn't as much hurt, like a parent might be, as he was disappointed—and I think that was what made me mad rather than remorseful. If he had come in with a different attitude, maybe I, in turn, would have responded differently. But he didn't, and he wasn't leaving—he just sat at my counter and drank his drink, smiling that ridiculous smile each time he asked a question or made a comment, as if that smile made everything he was doing okay. Not once during the conversation did I think that God might be speaking to me through this man's words; I mostly just thought he was a fraud and a bully. I finally told him that people like him were the reason it was so hard for me to trust Christians, or really to have anything to do with them at all. I told him that he should leave. He wouldn't, but continued talking as if I hadn't said a thing, or sitting in silence smiling at me. I could no longer process the conversation, and I started shouting at him to just get out.

His friend, the one who had come in with him earlier, tried to calm the situation down. He probably saved things from becoming any worse, if that was possible. He came up to the counter and said that we shouldn't be having this argument here, and that we should calm down—to which I replied, "If that's the case, then what was he thinking coming in here in first place?"

The guy was actually nice. He sort of apologized, and he asked to pray with me. I had no interest in praying at that point. At first, I allowed him to pray for the situation just to get him and his strange friend out of my shop and away from me. After a few minutes of praying, I could tell he was just a good guy trying to help the situation. We prayed, and they left. It was awkward and seemed like a strange way to end such an intense conversation that never had reached any resolution, but I was just glad it was over and hopeful God could at least salvage something out of it.

While all of this was going on, the regulars who had been there to visit me had come inside and listened to us argue. I became more and more upset at this, but there was nothing I could do—he had me cornered. After a while, they started to come up to the register and stare at me. At first I didn't realize what was going on; I was so focused on my argument that I didn't notice what they were trying to communicate. Each time one of them would come to the counter, I asked them what they needed, and they would simply say, "Nothing," and then continue to stare. Later, I found out that they were coming to the counter to ask if I wanted them to throw the guy out. Physically. He was harassing me, and they had had enough.

❂

Later, as I was outside sweeping and straightening the

front of the shop, some of those same regulars were out hanging around, sitting at tables and talking. When I first came out, they were all quiet. I stopped sweeping and just said to anyone who might be listening, "Not all Christians are like him. I hope you know that."

One of the guys sitting outside, we'll call him Tyson, said he understood that, but it didn't change the fact that he "still wanted to beat that guy's a--." I of course said that wasn't the way to solve anything, to which he replied that he knew that was how I felt ... "but Mark, sometimes people just have it coming."

As we were talking about the whole incident, who comes back to Java? Of course ... the pastor. He walked up to me and offered his hand, which I wasn't exactly interested in taking, but did anyway. What was I supposed to do? Part of me wanted to tell him to take his handshake and the damage he had already done and go back to Washington, but that wouldn't have solved anything. He apologized, and said that he should have come to me on his own instead of at the shop. When I looked around at the faces of the people who were watching this, I saw what I feared I would see: Yeah, right. I accepted his apology in the interest of making the whole mess go away, but it was too late for any damage control—like I said, the damage had been done.

He then took my phone number, which I had offered him before things got out of hand in the interest of bringing the whole scene to a close, and called me a couple days later, after his mission trip to Mexico. He asked me if I would meet him for coffee (no, not Java Jungle) and for whatever reason—who knows?—I said yes. I think part of it was my pride; I didn't want him to think he could intimidate me, but part of it was the side of me that can't let arguments like that remain unresolved. What followed was one of the strangest conversations I have ever had. We talked like two circling enemies, each of us keeping ev-

erything at a distance, stiff and suspicious. Back and forth.
Then he asked me what I thought he could do to reach
the youth of his congregation, and what my opinion on
youth ministry was. I don't know; I guess it was all a little
too weird. I don't even remember what I told him, because
I felt like the question came from out of nowhere, and I
wasn't prepared for it. I didn't feel qualified to have much
of an opinion on the subject. Maybe he was just trying to
communicate a respect for my opinion in the interest of
showing that his apology was sincere, or maybe he really
wanted help. (I honestly hope it was the former. I have no
idea how to run a church or youth group, but something
inside of me desperately wants to believe all pastors do. Too
much unintentional information. "You mean to tell me you
don't know? Who does? Anyone, anyone?" I mean, I had
just been screaming at this man a couple days ago when he
came in and tried to bury me with open-ended accusations
about my faith and my ethics.)

We stumbled through the conversation, and it ended with
the stiffest, most unnatural handshake ever.

This actually happened.

WHY?

That was just one story of so many that I could write
a few hundred books on the subject and not be finished
... I told it here because it truly was one of the proverbial
"last straws to break the camel's back"—the camel being
Stavesacre's desire (and my own) to continue our careers
within the industry that is called: the Christian Market.
The experience made it clear to me that the one thing left
to do, at least on our part, was to simply take us out of the
equation. The one error we could be held guilty of—biting
the hand that feeds—could be solved by simply not playing those shows ever again. I told this story to set a pace I
suppose, and also to deliver a point of the book you hold

in your hands from the beginning. Part of the reason I'm writing here is to explain why the collective members of Stavesacre no longer want anything to do with the Christian Market, and how we came to feel this way. There is a history to the way we feel, and I hope that will be enough to explain ourselves, because I've tried the direct approach, and it really doesn't tell the whole story.

Watch, I'll try it here: I think that the Gospel should be free, and that people who evangelize—with rare exception—shouldn't charge for it. I believe that people who assume that musicians are automatically preachers are mistaken. I can't find the term "role model," specifically as we Americans would define it, in the Bible. I believe that many of the musicians who call their bands a "ministry" have very little understanding of what ministry is. I believe that when God calls someone to a life of ministry, He provides for that person's needs—that person doesn't decide what a good profit margin for their ministry should be. I believe that the Christian Market is a security blanket that eventually smothers whoever hides behind it. I believe that many musicians who are very successful in the Christian Market would last exactly five minutes in the "general market"—a term only Christians use about the real world of Tower Records, MTV, and the good ol' radio—and that most of the bands who have tried the crossover have found their roles drastically changed from big fish in a wading pool to guppies in an ocean.

See? I could go on with these statements, and they would really do nothing to explain why I have come to feel this way ... or to correct the problem. And it is a problem. The Christian Market is not a "market" at all. It's people. It's primarily made up of God's people. And a group of individuals are making a living off of those people. They determine what is acceptable "Christian Living"—they tell us what God wants, usually based on what the majority of the people around them think—and then they market it, package it, and sell it at a premium. They even make a profit off of pointing out the Christians who are not living up to their market's standards, by finding a way to sell the idea that some people are just more like God, or "godly," than others. I want to show how I felt the same way at one point, how I blindly accepted some of the above errors as truths, and then by my own sin, found my whole outlook to be hollow and fruitless. I want to communicate that so many of the strange, and often damaging, situations Christian entertainers find themselves in come as a result of a so-called market that has tried to marry the finite wisdom of man with the infinite wisdom of God. I also want to show that by experience, I've found the whole concept to be flawed—Christianity as an industry is a conflict of interest.

Now, Stavesacre is just one band of five guys, and I am just one guy in the band. I am writing here on the assumption that you the reader might actually care to hear my opinion on this whole mess, and that's a little scary. I take some comfort in knowing no one really has to read all of this. I really don't have any idea what makes people care about bands, musicians, or artists. What makes someone a fan of the person behind the music as well as the music itself? (Much less read a book about that person's life?!) I don't understand why, when a person buys a record by another person, they suddenly find the desire to care what the person who made the record thinks about anything other than those songs ... but they do. I do. I am a fan. When I buy an album by someone, most of the time I would like to know where the person who made the music is coming from, and I guess that's why I feel that writing all of this isn't a colossal waste of time ...

Maybe we're all just trying to find out if we're alone, or if someone else out there feels the same as we do. I guess I'd like to know if that were true of my thoughts, that I might not be alone ... that would be good to know as well.

So. Here it is; let the boo-birds sing. I don't think everyone who reads this is going to be happy—that includes other musicians as well—and without apologizing for what I believe, I will offer this disclaimer: I'm not presenting this as "The Bible of Why You Shouldn't Support the Christian Industry" and definitely not as doctrine. It's just my outlook, my perspective. I sometimes use language that people don't agree with—for that I simply want to say that I will always write what is honest, including what I might wish wasn't.

I'm terrified that you'll be confused, so I hope you will forgive this brief little guide: This book is basically set up in two intertwined parts, and I have tried to weave them together where it makes the most sense to do so. There is the present, and the past. I am using the Stavesacre years to illustrate the present, and the other part—what I've been calling a "loose autobiography"—I am using to show how I got here. I don't really think about it as a study in contrast, but rather a reflection on cause and effect.

As far as what I hope to accomplish here ... I'm not just trying to tell you my life story. I am hoping to show you that the lives of the people who make music and entertain you are just as complex as yours. There are stories for our lives, too—ones that many people never see, and yet these people still feel at liberty to have all sorts of opinions about them. There are very real reasons why we do the things these people might be judgmental of, reasons that are true, honest, and righteous. Not everything is a step away from faith or backsliding, often the opposite is true, but many of us do what we believe is right, at the risk of being accused of those things anyway.

I guess in the back of my hope is the dream that maybe

we could be different from the world around us, that through actions as simple as how we treat each other, we could be witnesses as to who Jesus really is. We should at least be as good as the world around us, right? Shouldn't we, who claim to have what the world around us needs, treat each other with at least the same amount of common courtesy and love that they do? I would love to come off of a tour of nothing but clubs and bars and be able to say that I was glad to finally be around Christians again. As of right now … that is not the case.

If anything, maybe I could at least start a little dialogue between people, and maybe … just maybe, something will change.

I think we need it.

ONE

AN EXIT LETTER

This was the original title I had for this book, but I felt like it was a little bit too dramatic. I wrote this letter as we came home from a summer tour that had taken us through almost every Christian Festival and Christian Venue in the country. Just about the only festivals and shows we didn't play were dates we missed because our van broke down toward the end—a perfect way to finish a tour that nearly drove us all insane. I wrote this at about five in the morning, after driving all night from Texas, headed towards the West Coast ... headed home.

The letter itself is a bit dramatic (hey, it was 5 a.m., and I was over it), but I don't want to change it, because I'd like to keep my original feelings intact ... I want you to see what was on my mind, right then and there. I also wanted to see how much God would teach me during the writing of this book. I figured it might be a lot, seeing as we tend to learn about our own weaknesses and faults whenever we complain about someone else's.

Here goes ...

Lord, let me write. Let me write honestly. Let me write clearly. Let me glorify You in even this. Amen.

———————————————— ✦ ————————————————

It's been too safe
it's been too safe for too long
so little reaction, to good or bad
or right or wrong.
And I'm feeling restless here,
with "good intentions" and barbed wire
I want to go elsewhere
and set this place on fire.
NO ONE MOVE
we just wanna know
what's been waiting just outside
these walls are cold
from flames that give off only light
—I'm looking for heat
and sweat
and priceless tears of sincerity
can't be content
with less than everything
NO ONE MOVE
I wanna keep my eyes on You.
… set this place on fire.

"YOU KNOW HOW IT IS …"
Stavesacre, *Speakeasy*

———————————————— ✦ ————————————————

It's late. So late it's early, in fact. I just can't sleep. I can't sleep, and I can't stop thinking—bad combination at this hour. I can't sleep, so I write, and there you have it. We have just crossed the Arizona border, westbound on the 10. This isn't exactly the home stretch, but the end is in sight, and what a sight it is. We just finished the hardest, and, by most accounts, worst tour of our lives. Now we go home to start over. I hate saying that, "starting over." Every time I do, it sounds desperate. But it isn't desperate to me; it's just the truth. The fact that it feels desperate to me just shows me that I haven't really come to the place that I need to be: where all I care about is how I see me and how God sees me. The place where the only thing that matters is that I am where He wants me to be. It sounds so simple, just saying it in my head; it reads simple just looking at it on the page. I suppose that's just going to have to come in the course of my walk, my life. Is it that simple? I believe that at this point in my life, I am meant to find out.

What is this? The best way to describe it: This is one long letter that needed writing. It's a letter to you, the reader. If you have chosen to sacrifice some of those valuable minutes or hours that we as people of this new, busy, panic-filled, crucial time hold so dearly, then this is written with you in mind. True to form, I'm late. I have always felt that I could squeeze just a few more things into the time I had and, of course, won't hear any differently. Now the moment of need is upon me, and I choose now to start ... a little late. The ironic thing is, my tardiness may just be the thing that saves my skin and gives these last four or five years of heartache, trials, and tribulations the opportunity to be of some value beyond my own experience. You see, I think right now, but not a second later or even earlier, is the perfect time to say what needs to be said. Most of this will be written looking back on my life, looking back at memories I have purposely kept fresh in my mind. (To those friends who have had to hear some of these stories more than once or had to endure my venting for hours on end, thanks. See, some things really do have a higher purpose ...)

I write this letter to you on the verge of walking through a new, open door. I have no idea how long this door has been standing open; with all the nonsense I've been spending my time attending to, I wouldn't even have noticed until now. I am leaving behind a room I have spent too much time in, and I don't think I could write this if I had any intention but to leave. This room, and the world it represents, is a dead place. There's no good reason to be here; in fact, to stay would be unhealthy. It would be dishonest; it would lack the credibility you deserve from me, and then what would we have? More filler, more lies, more empty promises. I am a little uncertain of some things, but of the fact that we don't need any more nonsense—I could not be more certain.

You see, this is a letter of resignation. I am saying good-bye. Good-bye to all of you who like this old room, who can still live here and feel okay, still feel anything at all but the need to leave. I suppose this is a letter of warning, too. This old room is going to be the end of you; I do really believe that, if you choose to stay. This room is not a place that encourages or even values the things we are supposed to hold as precious and sacred. You should get out now, save what is worth saving—if in fact you can find anything of the sort—and get out. Get out and help with the gasoline and the matches.

Having said all that, I want to say that this is also a letter of hope. This old room is not a room at all, but a waste heap. It's a mire for pigs to wallow and root and suffer in. Hate to admit it, but the pigs here are you and I. But this is a letter about the hope that comes when you wake up one day and realize that although you have wasted so much of the precious time you've been given burying the "talents" (Matthew 25:25) God has given you in this mire, you don't have to stay here one moment longer. You can actually do something about the sinkhole you've slipped so far down into.

It's that kind of hope that is very much like the relief

you might feel once you realize you've been backing the wrong side. And knowing that side, knowing how that side treats all those guilty of treason, you find that it not only feels right to turn your back on it, but it feels even better to join the other side and start fighting the true good fight. Because the fact is: The side you've been backing is bad—probably evil.

It's a letter of hope and, believe it or not: joy. Can joy find a place in so much hurt, so much bitterness, and so much division? Yes, it can. Imagine how a slave might feel if he were to find out he's been free all along. I am free; I was a slave, but now I am free. I can find joy in that, and I truly hope that this letter will help some of my fellow slaves find joy as well. If it was ever there before, it can be found again. There are those who haven't ever had joy, or hope for that matter, but would dearly love to, and it's those people who I am leaving this old room to be with. Believe it or not, I believe that there—and maybe only there—I will find people who actually place value in the things that we have for so long self-righteously claimed to have exclusive rights. There is joy out there; it's rare—but when found, it's refined and held high as gold. Here, in this dusty, dry, old room, joy has been marketed, prostituted, and sold for a shameful pittance.

I am leaving. Good-bye. —July 27th, 2001

**... The sun is going down
I say we follow it out of town
—we've been here for far too long.
(but will they know we're gone?)
and in the morning, when it rises
maybe it will shine for us ...**

**"SUNDOWN MOTEL"
Stavesacre, *Speakeasy***

CHAPTER ONE

TWO

WHERE IT ALL BEGINS

I have two memories in my head that I think might be good places to start ... I guess I'll tell them both.

---✻---

It was lunch break, and I was heading out to "the Mall," the social hub of my high school, and for four years of my life, the center of the world. I was walking with my friend Wayne, the singer in the one and only band around town, made up of some other kids from the school. I had written a song, and I was looking forward to letting Wayne read my lyrics. He carried lyrics he had written during his lunch break (or in class) around with him in the same way that I, being an artist, always carried around a pad of drawings I worked on during my breaks (or in class) or on the bus. The idea of cruising around school with a song you had just written for your band seemed really amazing to me, and I wanted to try my hand at it.

I can still remember the song ... and I just might turn red

in the face remembering it, even while sitting here writing these pages all alone. The song was entitled "Forget It." (Yes, my face is, in fact, turning red.) I can't even remember the lyrics anymore; I just know they were probably extremely high and mighty, with a tone somewhere between a tough-and-jaded-yet-righteous-Christianity and still punk rock cool ... awful. I think the song was about one of those constant hot topics around campus at the time—abortion—and the lyrics went something like, Forget it ... Forget your baby ... blah, blah, etc. Cutting edge, non-compromising, and a bit ridiculous.

I gave Wayne the lyrics, and I swear, the moment they left my hands, I had the strangest feeling: These are bad ... awful, in fact. Too late. Wayne read quickly through them and handed them back to me.

"Well, what do you think?" I asked, looking up at him.

Pause.

"Uhh ... forget it."

We both laughed, in pity, for me.

Every morning, I rode the bus to school, and every day after school, I rode the bus home. The things we kids experienced ... trapped on that big bus only mildly supervised; freaking out in any possible way physically and emotionally—and often both, simultaneously—played a major role in my life. Those experiences shaped our troubled young minds, and it's probably a miracle that we all didn't go insane.

My longest running best friend John and I were often some of the last people to get off of the bus. John was the first person to befriend me when I moved to Madera. We met in the fifth grade and stayed fairly close throughout the next five or so years, going through a lot of those experiences together that hugely affect young kids' lives. He and

I discovered music together. (On one of John's birthdays, we both sat in awe listening to AC/DC's *Back in Black*, and soon after that, Soft Cell's "Tainted Love." Still later, as adolescents seeking identities, we both would walk down empty country roads with a handheld stereo listening to homemade punk rock compilations, then stay up late watching some of those early punk scene video classics like Suburbia and Another State Of Mind.) We became aware of girls together. (We both kissed girls for the first time within weeks of each other. I saw my first dirty movie at John's house. I got my little heart broken by a girl who he cursed as evil, right along with me, then turned around a couple of months later and dated.) We just sort of grew up together. We were as much best friends as kids who had just moved to a new place without many friends—right in the middle of discovering what friends were—or could be.

We were also friends in opposite worlds, and we had learned how to treat other people in completely differ-ent ways. My parents were strict, and while they had their hang-ups, they were never physically abusive. My mother is strong-willed; my stepfather's a good guy. By the time I met John, both of them had become devout Christians. John's parents were different. His mother was a gentle woman who was sort of run over by the men in her house. John was "the friend who cusses at his mom," which was really new to me. (If I had ever talked back to my mom the way he did every day, I would have found myself exiled to the bedroom, waiting out the storm of my mother's fury.) John told his mom to shut up. John told his mom, "No." John's step-dad, the other man in their house, was a cop who beat the hell out of both John and his mother. (It didn't matter who saw it either—I spent many uncomfortable afternoons hiding in John's bedroom, listening to the whole family go wild in the other rooms, only to have John come back into his room later and act like nothing had happened.)

As a kid, I didn't understand how much his upbringing had to do with the way John treated me and the other kids around him who actually cared about him. He made fun of anyone who might be a threat to his confidence, which was basically anyone who was close to him. The thing that hurt the most, though, was that due to a lot of my own experiences, I always looked for the friendship of people who withheld it. Ironically, I think the love my parents showed me left me a bit naïve as to the way the world was really going to be. (In response to that, I should probably beat my kids and treat my wife like dirt, right? Prepare them for the real world? I'm only kidding of course, but doesn't life always go 'round and 'round like that?) As any insecure kid would, I wanted John to think I was cool—that was the kind of acceptance a kid growing into himself needs from his friends—but John knew that, and so he used it to bolster his own lack of confidence and self worth. We were a bad combination; both of our screwed-up, young psyches complimented the unhealthier aspects of the other. My parents spent quite a few of their afternoons explaining that sometimes John just didn't realize he was being the way he was.

One late summer day while riding home on that accursed bus, in the inescapable heat of the San Joaquin Valley but blessedly near the end of the bus ride, John crushed me the way he often did. A parental counseling session was not far off.

Everyone else was stretched out comfortably in their own seats so they wouldn't have to touch the sweating arms of the kids next to them, but we were all sitting in the bench seats around John, and he was holding court. I was drawing in a notebook, while John talked nonstop with some of the other guys we ran with in those days. They were going on about a band they were starting, who was going to play what, what kind of music they were going to play, etc. I was attempting to draw them a logo. They weren't even a band yet—but all of the cool bands had logos or emblems ...

"Yeah, we're starting a band," John said.

What was that feeling in my stomach?

I nodded, keeping my eyes on the paper.

"Danny's gonna play guitar, Robert's gonna play drums, and we'll probably get some girl to play bass and sing. I'll play the keyboards."

Pause. Another nod from me.

"You're not in it."

The bus was quiet as the other kids looked at each other, hands held over mouths, giggling. I just nodded once more and kept looking at the paper.

If someone were able to bottle the courage that a kid has to show in order to not lose it when his most trusted friends try to intentionally make him lose it, that someone could probably rule the world.

———————————— ❋ ————————————

A young man is lost, mostly. If by God's grace he can find something he's good at—and find some success in whatever that is—it can provide for some much needed confidence. Unfortunately, young people tend to be cruel, and even the most confident kids can be jarred from their security blankets just long enough for the fools to get to them ...

FROM ALMOST NOTHING ... TO ALMOST SOMETHING

My parents used to be hell-raisers. That's the best way I can describe them from my memories of childhood. My mother once said that when I was a kid, she and my stepfather were mostly just parents "in theory."

My biological father and mother married shortly after she finished high school, pregnant with me. I was born in Reno, Nevada. We lived there until my grandparents drove through the rain and the hills and the night to pick up my mother, pregnant with my sister, and me to take us back to California with them. My "real father" had been busted a third time for selling drugs from out of our house. During the previous bust, the authorities told my mother they wouldn't let her keep me in that sort of environment, and so, this time, we finally left. To my memory, I haven't seen him since.

(My sister, fifteen years later and going through some good old-fashioned adolescence, tried to regain contact with him. After trading letters and information, he called the house. I actually spoke to him, and that was the last time we had any contact.)

Most of my memories of childhood are somewhat scattered, as I hope are most people's memories of childhood. (You remember in pieces, too, right? Right?) I remember being with my mom when she was single and my sister was just a little baby. I remember being robbed while living in an apartment that was beside some railroad tracks. I remember yelling into the floor-ducts of the air conditioning unit of my grandparents' house on my mother's side, and the returning echo of my own voice scaring me half to death. Swimming lessons, and summer days spent in my grandparents' pool. I remember my mother introducing my stepfather to my grandparents in the entryway of their house. I don't remember their reaction, but I know my grandparents; being introduced to the man my mother met at the Black Angus Bar and intended to marry was probably not something they saw as "good decision making," but yet another turn in the wrong direction. Ironically, this is the man who I would eventually come to think of as my dad. He was already divorced and the father of my soon-to-be stepbrother Jason; he was a biker/construction worker, and he was very similar to my so-called "real father." So as I said, he probably seemed like more of the same to my grandparents. Nevertheless, they were married soon enough, and from there, our real family began.

My parents have books and books of photos from those first years together. Lots of parties, and lots of crazy people hanging around. My dad was a carpenter, and most of his friends were the stereotypical '70s construction workers: loud, foul, and wild. I remember ... a motorcycle in the kitchen; discovering and then dismantling run-down appliances on the lawn in the backyard; exploring the alley behind our house. I remember playing with matches while staring in total ignorance at the graffiti and gang symbols in said alley. I have (sincerely) fond memories of my parents staying up with my aunts and uncles, playing cards and smoking ten thousand cigarettes until long after we kids went to bed. Bloodshot eyes in most of the photos. Beer, football, the dust from construction sites. Me with messed up hair and worn out clothes. Camping. I recall not recognizing my clean-shaven dad when he walked out of the kitchen after coming home from work, having shaved his beard for the first time since he had been known as "dad."

I had many great life experiences on both sides of my family. My dad's side of the family was always doing something together: Going to the beach was actually a common activity on both sides, but my dad's side of the family was just as likely to get all the aunts and uncles and respective children together for weekend camping trips and late nights around the campfires. There were cousins our age, so we had plenty of company. My parents liked a lot of the same activities that the aunts and uncles on my dad's side liked, so there was a kind of constant element of family around.

There was a lot of wild energy and wild behavior, and I was fascinated. A friend of my dad's, Bear, once said to me, "Mark, your old man is a tough S.O.B., but you just remember this: He don't chew glass like ol' Bear." It took my dad at least half of my childhood to convince me that Bear didn't actually chew pieces of glass.

We spent many weekends, especially during the summer, on the central California coasts of Pismo Beach, Morro Bay, and Santa Cruz. There was a lot of cold water, and there were long days on the sand. There were dune buggy trips (usually Volkswagen Bugs, stripped of their bodies and fitted with big sand tires, tail pipes, and roll-bars) and camp-outs. My dad's best friend, Paul, was once run over while out on the dunes. A buggy just ran right over him after he fell out of the one just ahead of it (he was fine). It was mostly fun, and always an adventure—maybe I wouldn't think so now, but as a kid, it was safe fun. "Hey, my dad does that all the time ..."

For example: I don't think it's still legal, and if it is, it probably shouldn't be, but my dad and his friends used to hang-glide. Hang-gliding was an extremely dangerous hobby that was popular when I was a kid. It involved a lightweight "glider"—essentially a man-sized kite—ropes, harnesses, and wind. The glider was made of a network of tin poles, nuts and bolts, and plastic material, all put together by the human beings willing to trust their lives with their kite-making skills. Once the glider was put together, the person would take it to a place that was nice and high, usually a cliff, and one that hopefully had a steady warm breeze blowing up its steepest face. The person would harness his body into the inner frame of the glider with ropes and clamps, point the glider downhill or toward the edge of the cliff face, and run full speed—carrying the whole apparatus—then jump off once he felt the wind begin to catch underneath the glider. Once airborne, the person strapped into the glider could steer—sort of—and sail like a bird. If the wind was right, one could stay airborne for quite some time, it would just take some warm air and a favorable breeze. One cold, central coast day, I watched my father, his friend Paul, and some of their other friends hang-glide through the fog on a central California beach, cliffs and all.

Surrounded by my mother and all of the girlfriends, wives, mothers, and other kids, we watched them shoot out of the fog, just above the rocky cliffs that are common on the central coast, then disappear into the fog again. This was normal behavior. (An early and related memory of unmatched, pure, childish jealousy: While hang-gliding off of El Kapitan peak in close-by Yosemite National Park was still legal, Paul once strapped his son Tyson, my childhood sidekick, to his back and took off from a cliff. The two of them sailed off through the sky. I watched from the edge, and made my dad promise he would take me sometime. "Maybe ... next time." Never happened. Tyson was about three or four years old and weighed about one third of what I did ...)

I look back at those days with a definite sense of comfortable nostalgia. The song "Sand Dollar"—named for the shells we used to find on the beach in Morro Bay—off of Stavesacre's second album, *Absolutes*, was partly a look back on those days. I think that when I wrote it, I was looking for some perspective on my life, by holding it up against the contrast of those early years.

The sun, the air,
the faithful crashing waves.
Carefree, comforted,
knowing eyes watched over me.
Even now I taste the salt on my lips,
skin dried by the sun,
an ocean limitless ...
taking me back,
to better days ... that seem so far away.
Somehow, somewhere,
I've lost a part of me.
Got caught up in this twisted place,
and I lost simplicity.

CHAPTER TWO

The things I've seen have tainted everything,
I think I gave up living ...
When life is stained, can it be cleaned?
Want to know, if I can
Set aright a life that's gone so wrong?
In a way, start again ...
if not what is left?
If I could do it on my own,
I'd have done it long ago
I'm sure that I have tried ...
The sun, the air,
the faithful crashing waves.
remind me of a child that I'd love to be again.
Only now, finding comfort and peace
in trusting a God of even more than I might see.
And even more ... than better days.
To trust again ...

"SAND DOLLAR"
Stavesacre, *Absolutes*

It was a simpler time, and, held up against the life I have
now and the things I know, I almost feel like I was a lot
closer to being the ideal Christian man that I am constantly
aware—and made aware—that I'm not.

A NICE BIG CLOSET FOR ALL THE SKELETONS

Not all of those memories were fond, of course.

One of my dad's friends, while in a drunken rage and
probably wildly high on amphetamines, beat and then
chased his wife—one last time—through their house. She
had to shoot him many times before he finally ran out of
whatever it was that kept him coming after her. The photos
in our family albums of those house parties my parents put

on or attended were full of people with bloodshot eyes and cloudy looks on their faces for a reason: Heavy drug and alcohol use were just part of the landscape. The presence of drug abuse and subtle racism were just as common as divorce or drunkenness amongst a lot of the crowd that made up the scene my parents hung around. Drugs weren't the evil then that they are known to be now, although it's difficult to look back at the way everything was—dirty, disheveled, out of control—and understand how the truth wasn't obvious to everyone.

Our family was not without it's share of madness.

On Christmas and Thanksgiving, we would always make the rounds to each side of the respective families: Mornings would usually be spent on my mom's side; evenings would be spent on my dad's side. We would gather at both respective grandparents' homes, and there would be relatives whom I hadn't seen all year. (Or sometimes had never met. My dad's family was huge, and it always seemed like I was meeting new cousins, aunts, and uncles, etc.) These gatherings were often good for a little glimpse into the complicated, and sometimes very dark, network of our families.

One Christmas night, or some family holiday, we were all gathered at my grandparents' house on my father's side. We had already opened all of the presents, ate all of the food, and discovered (whether we realized it or not) that no toy was as much fun as conversation. It was in the later part of the evening that my grandparents would always get phone calls from all over the country from those relatives who couldn't make it, wouldn't be coming out to California this year, etc. My grandmother would always sit right by the phone and field the calls, then pass on whatever greeting the family on the other end wanted passed on to either my grandfather or the whole family. That night, one of my aunts called, very distressed. Her husband was bad, and he was bad right then. We kids were sitting around my grandmother and could hear everything she was saying. We looked at each other, then at all of our parents' expressions, and we could tell something was not right.

My grandmother became very upset and told my grandfather what was going on. Apparently, my aunt's husband was going to kill her, or hurt her badly. (Is there really a difference between the two, to a bunch of wide-eyed kids watching their grandmother cry?) She was carrying on and on about it, right at that moment. Whenever my grandmother would pull the phone away from her ear, we could hear our aunt yelling through the earpiece.

When my grandmother told him, my grandfather nearly exploded right there in front of all of us. I remember seeing him jump up from his chair and head to the bedroom, yelling at my grandmother to tell our aunt to pass on some information to her crazy husband: "You tell that S.O.B. that I'm going to get my gun!" My grandmother was completely freaked out already, but when she saw my gramps, who had had heart surgery a few years before, dead serious and jumping up from his chair, she lost it, too. Eventually, some of the family went to my aunt's house and settled everything—all the guns stayed in their resting places.

One night a couple of my cousins—who lived in a side house next to the house their parents lived in, which served as their party place and also storage for car parts and tires—crashed their car into a telephone pole/power line. The driver got out and inspected the damage, then in frustration and anger pounded the hood of the car and was electrocuted and killed.

Apparently, the power line had fallen over the car and was touching part of its frame. This same family was later found to be supplying truckers and members of my family with Crystal-meth and other drugs.

This is where things start to get a little too close, and where feelings could get hurt. I can talk about some things that are a little way out from my immediate family, but anything closer would be crossing a line that I happen to enjoy the existence of, and so I'll leave the family business where it is—in the family. Besides, I'm sure some of the stories of those days will eventually rise and surface in some fashion later on in my life—who knows?—but I think my family portrait is well painted.

I spent the night in homes I had no business spending the night in, waking the next morning to find naked people walking around doing naked people things. I was allowed to play at homes that I would never have allowed myself to play at, where gangs and drugs were part of the normal landscape of so many friends and family members that I grew up thinking of those elements as normal. Somehow, my fears weren't about the police raiding my house, guns being wielded at me by my parents, or gangs jumping me in. In their own way, those types of things seemed comical to me, like watching television. (I didn't live in a war torn city, or a place that was dramatic enough to make movies about, but I lived in one where reality was unkind enough for me to recognize that I had it good.) The things that I experienced right outside my door weren't as much normal in my home, as they were normal in the world around it. Even a kid knows that some things are just not right, but he also knows they aren't his fault. I had other worries. When you're a kid, your perspective allows for thoughts like, "Wow, his big brother just threw him all the way across the room. I can't leave now—I'm too busy trying to pretend that I didn't see it happen. I wonder how much trouble I'm going to be in for coming home after the street lights come on?"

For a little kid, getting into trouble for coming home late takes on a whole new life when your parents aren't sober or rational. I didn't fear them as much as I feared what I couldn't understand: mood swings at home and parents whose personalities seemed to change for no reason at all. It would literally take hours for me to get the courage to come around my mother or father if I had gotten into trouble, for fear of strangely cold words and outbursts of anger. Later, after learning about the effects of alcohol abuse and drug use, all of that made more sense to me, but at that age, I was just worried that my mom didn't like me. For a child, the chemical factor never comes to mind. Sometimes I would be in trouble, and I could feel an absence of forgiveness and disappointment in my parents' body language. I would see the clenched teeth and furrowed brows, and I would spend the rest of the day hiding away in hopes of avoiding another freezing stare. Then, other times, I would get into trouble, and there would be no mistaking the forgiveness and the love. It followed no pattern that I could identify, so it was confusing.

I've seen some of my best friends beaten in their kitchens and bedrooms, cowering in corners, or screaming in rage at drunken fathers who have had a bad day. Given what appears to be an automatic assumption by society around us—abuse happens at home for the working class—I guess I should be thankful that amazingly, divinely, that was never me. My dad was a tough guy early on, but he had character even then. Sure, I got smacked on the backside my fair share of times, but I never experienced the abuse that I saw my friends or some of my relatives go through. I'm sure there were plenty of spankings that were more anger and lashing out than the kinds of spankings that kids just get, but believe me, you learn the difference. I was never afraid of getting hurt; I was more terrified of all of the yelling and arguing between my parents or relatives and then the resulting quiet around the house afterward. (I have to say, though: I always thought the foul language was sort of funny.) Most

of all, I was afraid of that deafening silence. When the yelling and the cursing stopped, I always dreaded the hours that
it would take for things to get back to the way I liked them:
happy. There was such a swing between atmospheres in the
house. One day everyone would be having the time of their
lives and making for good memories—good times!—but
the next day could see the same family in a completely
different, darker light. I think the worst of those early days
were the cold stares and the feeling that my parents could
change into people I didn't recognize in an instant.

Not all of the memories were fond, but I suppose given
the circumstances, they could have been worlds worse.

Recently, while looking through some old photo books, I
saw a picture of my mother sitting on the floor in my dad's
parents' living room, the house we lived in for the first half
of my childhood. She looked so young, and somehow different. My mother was looking at the pictures with me, and
as my dad and I commented on the photo of her, she said,
"Yeah. That was right after I had your sister. I was doing a
lot of speed then."

!

I ... don't think I can really describe the way it felt to hear
something like that now, after all of the time that has passed
since those days. I was shocked, but not shocked. I have
known that my parents did drugs for a long time, and I
clearly remember that there was a lot of drinking going on.
It's just always strange to hear my parents, the parents that
I know now, talk about those days in their past. It doesn't
happen often, but of course (like bad solo albums), there
is always someone or something around to keep you from
forgetting entirely.

My mom and my stepfather got married in Reno, and
the photo of that blessed event is the most hilarious thing. I

CHAPTER TWO

love to tease them about it: hippie/biker shirts, white with lace and frills; my dad with his dead-on Superfly haircut, big mustache, sideburns, and all; and both of their eyes nearly shut, completely bloodshot.

Like I said, my parents were hell-raisers.

But then that chapter ended. As I have said in many im-promptu counseling sessions around the fire pit in the back-yard of my current house, my parents became the kind of conservatives that former hell-raisers become, and strangely enough, that's when all of the confusing parts start.

As long as I can remember, I've felt the need to put what was in my head down on paper. I don't know when I start-ed to show an artistic side—my mother has pictures that I scribbled from so long ago I have no recollection of ever drawing them. (That seems so weird to me. Like someone else did them or something ...) Some part of my brain can at least make a slight connection with most of the pictures, paintings, and songs that I've done, but none of what my mother has shown me even registers. Whatever was on the mind usually finds its way to the page. When I was little, ap-parently my brain only had time for Batman and monsters. Spidey was probably too complicated. (While most kids were out riding bikes or learning how to skateboard, I was in my room, drawing pictures. And I hated tracing; I always wanted to do my own versions of the heroes and villains I saw in my comic books. Besides, that was cheating.)

I do remember how proud I was of the pictures I fin-ished. I loved to see the whole page come together; I loved to see everything in its place. I didn't know how to define that then, but now I know that I loved to find the theme of a picture, whether that theme was found in the colors I used or the story I could tell from the finished image on the page. Sometimes—often—I couldn't finish a picture simply because I knew that when all of the ideas in my head were out, it wouldn't look right. I think that strange conviction played a major role later in my life ... all the way to what you are reading now.

I found a lot of my confidence as a boy though art, and that side of me has remained consistent. I grew up with it. (First drawing pictures, then singing songs, and now it looks like long, rambling ... "letters.")

THEN, THE WHOLE WORLD CHANGED

My parents bought some land out in a part of Madera County known as "the Ranchos" early on in their marriage. My earliest memory of it was going out to "the house" before there was a house there at all, and breaking the ground with my parents and my aunt and uncle—my mother's sister and her then husband—and planting a living Christmas tree. It was cold and windy, and my mother was wearing a green and white jacket that I will probably always associate with that part of my life.

We had to go out to the property on Saturdays—and sometimes on Sundays—to "help" my dad build the place.

Torture. Saturday's are cartoon days, obviously.

Once we got out there, it was usually worth it. There were always adventures for us in the open fields and around the house and property. Not many people lived out there then, and even now it's still not considered a city, just a steady stream of people building and developing.

I believe the intentions my parents had when buying that property were probably far different from the reasons they were glad we moved there once we did. At first it probably seemed like a nice place to live, good investment, own your own land and house, etc. Then the whole world changed for my family and me: My dad became "born-again" when I was about ten years old. My mother did the same shortly after. Suddenly, living out there, I believe, looked like a way to start life over.

One of my uncles on my mother's side—her oldest brother—was the man I have always remembered as my first experience with true Christianity. God used him to lead my dad to Him, and still today he remains a consistent example of a truly "godly" man. My dad listened to the radio a lot in those days, and there was a man named Chuck Smith who God also used, through a program from southern California that was broadcast all the way up in Fresno and even out into the Ranchos. My dad started talking differently, and acting differently, and so did my mom. The nights of card playing and parties were mostly gone. The language had already been changing—I think my parents felt the need for change in our family for the sake of our future. Before my dad got "saved," they both had already stopped smoking and drinking, and just before we got serious about building the house, most of the related behavior had faded out completely. We started going to a little Baptist church and became involved in the community. I even started meeting kids out there at the church. If I remember correctly, my dad even helped build the church itself, which was just around the corner and down the street from our house.

I don't believe that my parents became Christians because that was part of their new take on life. I think if anything, the changes had begun because God had been drawing them toward Him for some time, and that was just their way of "waking up" (or maybe better, "coming back from the dead") spiritually.

Their best friends, Paul and his wife Karen, had also moved out to the country. They even lived on the same block, and they had sort of calmed down, too. The difference between the two couples was made obvious though, mostly by the fact that as soon as my parents became Christians, our families spent less and less time together, and eventually we completely drifted apart. My parents truly were no longer walking the same path as the majority of their peers, and it was obvious that it had less to do with something they decided to do, but more as a result of a change that happened to them.

We were there for about two years. I remember vacation Bible study, potluck dinners, and yellow windows.

YELLOW WINDOWS

I was standing next to my mother and father while the congregation meandered through an old hymn that we had probably sang about a million times. I remember the yellow "stained glass" windows that, while not stained glass at all, just plastic, sure were yellow. Coupled with the ever-present dust that was a signature item of the Ranchos, I will forever associate my brief time at that church with yellow-plastic-window-tinted air. I usually hated those windows; they made me feel trapped and ... stuffy.

But this day, I didn't feel trapped at all.

As a matter of fact, I felt wonderful.

This time, my mind wasn't wandering all through the atmosphere, bored to near insanity and jealous of the kids that got to draw pictures on the pamphlets they gave us when we walked in. I wasn't wondering what the people outside were doing. I wasn't staring at the baptismal behind the pulpit, wondering if and when I would finally get to swim in that thing during church, like I had seen other people do on a few occasions.

This time, I had my head hung down, and I was staring at the back of the pew in front of me. I was listening to the words of old Al, the first preacher I had ever met. I don't remember what he said, I just remember that during the "invitation"—or altar call, where the pastor asks if anyone would like to come forward—without warning, I started walking up to the front of the church. I don't remember crying or anything; I just remember my feet. I still to this day believe that I didn't have complete control of them. Say what you want to, but that's my memory, and I stand by it. It's one of the few memories I have of that far back in my life, but it's still clear in my head ... Looking down at my feet as they marched up to the front of the church ... then the short carpet getting really close to my face as I knelt at the steps of the pulpit ...

And that was it.

I believe that although I may not have fully understood what had happened to me, God saved me that day. I have strayed, I have wandered, I have stumbled, but through it all, that memory has always stayed with me. From that moment on, I do believe I have always known the truth.

Yellow windows.

NEW CONFLICTS

We attended the Baptist church long enough to befriend some members of the congregation and become a part of our community. My parents got involved; there were planning sessions, "get-togethers," outreaches, etc. Our old pastor, the "Reverend Al"—kind of creepy, what with the black smoker's-gums and flattop haircut—eventually retired from the ministry, and another pastor was elected by the elders. He was everything that Al was not, and that wasn't such a good thing. He was young and had plenty of charisma, and he was full of energy and ideas. Al liked things the way they were. Al was sort of a "good ol' boy," so no, he probably was not the best man for the job. But he did care about us. And he at least seemed to grasp the fundamentals of the scripture, however flawed he may have been. Even the most charismatic personality in the world still isn't enough to substitute for sound doctrine, and my parents and many of the people in the church body learned that the hard way.

It had become apparent that the new pastor had some

beliefs that were quite different from those we had been practicing. My dad confronted the pastor on issues of doctrine, particularly the validity of Scripture. There had been some debate between them regarding the Bible and its infallibility. My dad believed that it was all still relevant; the pastor apparently believed not all Scripture still held true today. My dad didn't talk about it much; he just followed his convictions—meaning, he followed what he believed was true and how far he would allow that concept of right and wrong to dictate his actions.

The confrontation didn't have the kind of results that my dad could agree with, so he had to trust his convictions further and take the debate to a higher intensity. He went through the process that Jesus gives us to follow in Matthew 18:15-17 regarding a brother sinning against you, taking a couple of elders from the church aside with him to confront the pastor. I don't know how that meeting went, who sided with whom, but what I do know is that soon after, our whole family was standing in front of the congregation. My dad told them that we would no longer be attending the church on the grounds that false doctrine was being taught there. There was crying and whispering, people looking at each other in unspoken surprise, shared sadness, and even agreement with the things my dad was saying. Some of members of the congregation were looking at each other with what even I could see was quiet satisfaction; not everyone was sad to see us go. I remember crying because it was emotional, and I was a little kid, but I also remember thinking to myself that I really didn't know why I was crying, since I didn't like that church much anyway. Goodbye new pastor, goodbye ugly yellow windows.

We spent some time checking out different churches. I really only remember one church that we tried, one I later learned to be "charismatic"—an entirely different charisma than that of the newest pastor at the good ol' Baptist church. You have to understand that as a family who really had had no interaction with any Christians other than those at our quiet little church in the middle of nowhere, a big charismatic church is a completely different world. I would like to be gentle in recounting the experience, but I also have to stay true to how I felt that day, knowing what I knew about Christianity at the time. I think we probably stayed for the whole service, but I'm sure my parents would just as likely have run out of there with us wrapped over shoulder and under arm. There were people yelling, waving their hands in the air, and jumping around. People—who were, as far as I knew, mumbling and saying words that I couldn't understand, over and over—surrounded me. It was scary for us—that's just the truth. Now, learning more about the movement, I have a bit more understanding, but I guess I just can't deny the way I felt as a little kid in a church full of people doing things I had never seen before.

Having had my first experience with it as a person who had just been introduced to Christianity, if I find myself in that kind of setting, I can't help but wonder if there are any other people in the room who are right where I was as a kid, and how they must be feeling. When I read 1 Corinthians 14, verse 23, "...Therefore, if the whole church comes together in one place, and all speak with tongues, and there come in those who are uninformed or unbelievers, will they not say that you are out of your mind? ..." (NKJV) I am comforted. The message of that passage—order, and maybe some humility—seems clear to me, but if I ever bring it up to someone who feels at home in an environment like the one I just mentioned, the conversation always gets a lot more intense. I just can't shake the feeling that they're trying very hard to justify emotionally charged behavior. I admit that I don't know everything, and I'm open to discussion on this topic now, but as a kid who was totally new to the experience, there was no room or time for a conversation about something so complicated. I was scared to death, and so were my parents.

We didn't go back.

NEW HOMES

An aunt invited us to a church back in Fresno called Calvary Chapel. This church was a branch of a much larger church body in Southern California, Calvary Chapel of Costa Mesa, and of which the man I mentioned earlier, Chuck Smith—who my dad was listening to on the radio—was the head pastor. We went one morning and immediately felt at home. The music was unreal, compared to the dusty, old, bare-boned hymns we were used to, and the guys singing and playing reminded me of some of the music my parents raised us on. (Compared to our first church, the Calvary style of "worship," a new term to me then, was the polar opposite of what we were used to ...) The pastor spoke in terms that my parents could understand, and respect. I could tell that they felt comfortable, and after attending a few weeks, I knew it was going to be our church.

When we first started attending, Calvary Chapel of Fresno met at the American Legion Hall on First Street. There were people everywhere in the main hall where church services were held—people sitting on folding chairs, on the stage in the back of the room (where my friends and I eventually sat once we were old enough to sit wherever we wanted), and on tall stools all along the walls. After church, we would go into the cafeteria across the hallway to the back of the Legion Hall. It was huge to me then. Driving by there now, I can hardly believe it was ever big enough to hold all of us. It's taken on a sort of mythical role in my memory as being bigger on the inside than on the outside, like the wardrobe in Lewis' *Narnia* series. I also remember it having a dull, foul smell, like sour milk. I now know that smell as used liquor ...

THREE

WHERE IT ALL CONTINUES

Shortly after our family finally settled on a home church, I began the difficult journey of being raised in a Christian home by two people who had not grown up in the same manner, having only been introduced to Christianity much later in their lives as parents and married people. That part of my life began at about the age of nine or ten, and I, of course, had no idea what lay ahead of me: adolescence, junior high and high school, society, and then eventually, coming of age, in a world very much different than the one my parents had just begun raising me in. I believe they loved me, my sister, and our stepbrother Jason, and that they did the best they could with what information and experience they had. Seeking guidance from the Holy Spirit and the Scriptures, they tried to steer us away from the lives they lived and mistakes they made, attempting to shelter us from the harsher side of life they experienced.

The problem with sheltering children is that, as far as I've ever seen, it never works the way people think it will. It may have changed the way we were going to learn about life, and it certainly protected us from a lot, but it also added a whole new set of problems, a whole new divide separating children from parents. We already had the generation gap to deal with …

I had some trouble my middle school years, and I think my parents were really afraid that I was going in the wrong direction. To make the bad decisions I was making, right before I started a period of my life when would be most susceptible to bad influences, worried them a lot.

I lied all of the time, mostly about schoolwork. It wasn't that I struggled with learning or studying; I just didn't want to do it. Schoolwork was boring to me, and I was stubborn. I got into the habit of not doing anything that I thought I could avoid. If my parents asked me about something like homework, I would just lie, and the inconvenience of a math assignment or a book report would just go away until the last minute—when I had to do them.

I lied about schoolwork, but I also lied about things that I thought might get me into trouble. The problem with all of this lying was the same problem that I had with anything I would try to get away with—my parents always caught me. That's what happens when your parents have already done everything you might even think about doing, and gotten away with it. They can't remember any of the details of the trouble they got into—oh no, of course not—but they can remember all of the methods they used to avoid getting caught, and they have no problem remembering the signs that would give a would-be troublemaker away.

I don't know if they just saw it all happening, allowed me to get into the trouble, then caught me at the last minute, or if they were just good detectives. One way or another, though we had our differences, they were good parents, and that's a beautiful thing. They weren't perfect (a standard to which, growing up, and even as an adult, I had a hard time not holding them to) but they cared, and that means everything.

THE TRASH CAN

One fine Saturday afternoon at the end of my seventh grade school year, a friend of mine named Eric and I went to a local grade school to watch some of the Little League games that were played there every weekend. We hung around and did what most kids do on a Saturday afternoon: nothing. We watched a few of the games, but neither of us really cared about baseball, so we went cruising through the school buildings, walking the outside halls, and basically just killing time around the yards. After a while, Eric and I went into the boys bathroom and made a bunch of racket, the kind young and dumb kids make: yelling, slamming doors, scratching our names into stall walls, etc.

As I came out of one of the bathroom stalls, I noticed Eric had started a small fire with some paper towels, and was waving the burning paper towels around the bathroom. Being fascinated with fire as all young and dumb kids are, I wanted to start a little fire of my own. As I rolled up pieces of toilet tissue (obviously to pretend I was smoking a giant Bob Marley style joint—oh yeah, don't do drugs, kids,) Eric started another fire on a completely different level: the trash can. He was burning papers inside the can, and the flames grew high, very quickly.

Eric and I started to panic, seeing as we could actually hear the papers burning in the can—deep down inside the can—so we wedged it inside a urinal and started flushing. While Eric flushed, I cupped water in my hands and dumped it into the trash can, hoping that with all the water, the papers would just have to go out.

They would just have to.

Finally, the flames disappeared, and we claimed victory.

We left the bathroom feeling like outlaws who had just narrowly escaped the sheriff and his posse. We were ten feet tall and wanted everyone to notice. As we passed a young kid named Patrick, we bragged, "We just set some fires in the bathroom! They were burning' all out of control ... but we stopped them ... It was sooo coool!" (Hey, look. I was an idiot kid. We do things like that. The fact that I didn't kill myself about a hundred times acting like this has to be worth something, right? Right?) We left Patrick—visibly amazed at our bravery—and went back over to the baseball games where we could sit on our bikes and look as cool as we felt.

At home later that day, my dad pulled me aside. He had a very serious look on his face.

"Son, I need to ask you a question," he said.

"Okay," I replied, completely clueless as to what this was all about.

"Were you at the school today?" he asked.

"Well, yeah. I was there with Eric. We were watching the games."

"Did you use the boy's bathroom at the school?" he asked. Now I understand.

"No, Dad, why?" I lied.

"Well, today there were three fire engines and four police cars at the school. Someone pretty much burned the boys' bathroom down. There were police everywhere. There were a lot of little kids around the school; a lot of people were pretty worried. I'm just glad you're okay, and that you didn't have anything to do with it."

Terror.

That night after dinner, I called Eric, and we met for a little planning session at the school. We came up with a story, but I had a sick feeling in my stomach. I'd never escaped this sort of situation before; I guess I hoped this one was so absurd I might just pull it off.

I sat on my lie and forgot the whole thing.

The next week, I was at school, sitting in my hot and muggy classroom, the knowledge that summer was just around the corner making it nearly impossible to sit still or not watch the second hand go slowly around the clock. (I swear, they put those big huge clocks in schools on purpose, maybe for revenge. Torture. I don't know ...) Then the principal's voice came over the P.A. that went out over every classroom, calling me into the office, and I froze in my seat. Suddenly it was not so much hot and muggy in the classroom as it was boiling and freezing at the same time, right where I sat. I made my way to the principal's office, in a daze. I came right out of my daze though, when I turned the corner in the hallway that led to the office and saw a policeman, a man in a suit, and Eric sitting with the school principal in his office. Yeah, I came right out of that daze.

Well, of course, we were found out. I told the whole story exactly as it happened, especially when I was told not to lie, and that Eric had "... already told us all we need to know." As it turns out, little ol' Patrick What's-His-Name was the son of Fire Marshall What's-His-Name, and the poor little kid was so freaked out that he went and told his father everything.

For my brave acts, I received a meeting with my mother and my very first Juvenile Discipline Coordinator, as well as an entire summer of Saturdays—twice as long as Eric because he could skip church to work on Sundays, which I was not allowed to do—picking up trash, pulling weeds, and removing large dirt-clods from future parking lots, all for the city of Madera. It was either that or two months in Juvenile Hall, and my mother was having exactly none of that. (I think the whole "two months" threat might have been a total lie on the part of the Discipline Coordinator, designed to scare the hell—literally—out of kids like me. Yes, it worked.) Nothing like backbreaking labor without pay to make a kid rethink himself. I also spent a good two or three days cleaning and scrubbing the boys' bathroom, which was covered in an inch of soot. The garbage in the can had not only not gone out, but had caught the can itself on fire. The trash can was made of hard plastic and had burned slowly and steadily in the bathroom with the door closed, with only a small vent near the bottom of the bathroom door to allow the smoke out. The last thing we removed from the bathroom was the small mound of plastic that had been a full-sized Rubbermaid trash can.

Now, all of that was awful, but none of it came close to actually facing my dad when I had been found out. At the time, I would have tripled my "work detail" if it meant not having to admit to my dad, again, that I had lied. Forget the fire—I knew it was the lie I would be in trouble for, and that caused me the most stress in the whole ordeal. I didn't have any idea what would happen, but I also didn't have any idea what I would learn, or how my dad would surprise me into changing the course of probably the rest of my life.

He picked me up from school and let me know that whatever after school activity I had planned was now canceled, and we rode in silence for some time. When we finally got home, we sat in his truck, with the keys still in the ignition—I never took my eyes off of them—and my dad just sort of sat back in his seat in a posture that says, "Soon we will have, a talk."

We talked for a minute about everything, and I admitted what I had done. It was then that he cut me off and said the one piece of profanity that I have ever heard him say since I learned what a Christian was and that he was one of them.

"... I'm sorry I did that, Dad. I know it was wrong, and—"

"Mark. It's not what you've done." he said, cutting me off. "It's not the fire, or any of that. It's the d----- lies. You've got to stop the lies."

Uh-oh.

"Go to your room. I'll be in there in a little while."

Now, my father believed in spankings and groundings. That's it. That's the deal. And I believed in them, too; I still do. My father never punched me in a drunken rage or burned me with lit cigarettes. He believed that discipline would make us aware that we had done something wrong. But there are two ways you can be made to feel bad about what you've done: You can feel honest remorse when shown that your actions were wrong, or you can be made to feel like you are worthless for doing something that isn't perfect. My situation was the first. My dad was going to give me a spanking, a grounding, or both. It was a simple reality, and I was still young enough to understand what it meant.

As I lay in my room, I think I really did ask God to kill me. "Just take me now. I'm willing. Go ahead, anything but this." Anything but being in trouble, and having my parents disappointed in me. I felt such remorse, and my dad's words just kept echoing in my head, morphing into different tones of sincerity, "It's the d----- lies ...The D----- Lies ...THE D----- LIES ..."

When my dad finally came into my room, he sat down on the edge of the bed and asked me a question I hadn't prepared myself for.

"Son, do you know how much it hurts me when you lie to me?"

I said no.

"Do you know how it makes me feel to have to discipline you?"

No again. Sort of crying now.

"Well, I want you to know how it feels, and how much it hurts me, when you give me no choice."

My dad got off of the bed, and got on his knees.

He took off his shirt, and laid it on the floor. Then he

handed me his belt. "Okay son, now I want you to use that belt on my back, and tell me how it feels."

I immediately burst into tears and begged him not to make me do it. He wouldn't give in until I tried, bringing the belt down on his back one time in more of a falling motion, rather than a hitting motion, and that was all that I could do. He knew that I got the point, and it was over.

I'm a grown man now, but I fall back on the wisdom I gained through this experience often. I learned a whole lot about right and wrong, lying, my parents, and even God.

Now, did I lie again? Probably. Did I lie the way I used too? No way.

It's like I said, they cared, and that means everything.

When I moved on to junior high, I was introduced to a man whose impact on my life I have a hard time measuring, even now. His name was Cary Wendell, and next to my parents and my uncle, he was probably the biggest influence on my spiritual maturity. He became that by living out many of the characteristics we are all expected to show according to the Bible: He was loving, gentle, and long-suffering. He challenged me concerning my own responsibility, and how not following through with my responsibilities actually affected other people, people like him.

He first began discipling me while I was in junior high. Because of him, discipling was a term that I was introduced to in it's proper light: with time, honesty, and consistency. The hard things. Discipling is not eloquently worded speeches that sound inspiring to those who might be listening in or those who worship the ground the speaker walks on. Discipling is also not workbooks and programs that take little time or heart to follow and that are less ministry tools, but more revised school curriculums.

When he came to our church, he had just graduated from Biola University and was a new face in a small crowd of people. Not too much later he was appointed the role of "youth leader," and he really seemed to enjoy the thought of injecting some life into a small and bored group of young people. I was one of the oldest kids at the church, and he and I became friends easily. He wasn't this overbearing personality, but instead, he was just a laid back, quiet individual. My parents asked me if I would be interested in him coming over and discipling me after school one day a week, and I agreed, mostly because I didn't want to upset them. Soon I was into it on my own, because Cary was cool, and he seemed to really want to be involved in my life. I didn't understand why, but it also never really occurred to me to ask. (That seems strange to me now, but back then, I was a lot less skeptical of everyone, and I never gave it much thought.)

For a few years, from junior high through most of high school, Cary came over once a week after school and talked to me about God and my faith. We talked about other subjects, mostly music and the girls I was never going to get to talk to me, and we did a lot with the other kids in the youth group. I think he just wanted to nudge me along, encourage me. He used to ask me the hardest questions though, because they all had this sort of humbling, searching quality about them. I learned a lot in those days, and while I may not remember the specifics, I do feel like I absorbed the intent and the motivation of Christianity. From him, I learned that motives are far more important than outcomes. He didn't teach me what it meant to be Christlike by anything less than the way he lived his life, and I'd say getting a kid to even care about something like that was a huge accomplishment.

The lessons I learned from Cary were more from experience than actual words. They were from things that can't be learned on a sidewalk, being cornered by some person who is trying to build up "treasures in heaven" by giving me a tract or by carrying around an actual wooden cross with scripture verses scrawled on it in black felt tip pen, from a Bible I may or may not have ever read. I learned that care and attentiveness to the details of my life were the way to my respect, and ultimately my attention.

Cary was there when my ex-girlfriend died of a brain hemorrhage. He was there when I burned all of my records, attempting to free myself from what I was made to believe was "bondage" in my life. He was there when I couldn't talk to my parents.

Even when I faded a bit in my zeal for learning, Cary kept coming around. I'm sure he continued to pray for me.

Recurring theme: He was there. This is what I have come to trust, even more so now that I have been around so many people who were not willing to do the same, including myself.

HIGH SCHOOL

My high school years were nothing like I expected.

I had been warned by my parents a million times over that I shouldn't miss out on anything. I had heard and witnessed the subtle lament of so many people who thought that high school was the last time they were truly able to feel free. I got the hint from the television shows, songs, movies, and all of the other things in our media-based culture that pointed to a time when so many people still claimed they had a chance to "be who they always wanted to be." I went through high school determined to never say things like that, or regret the way I spent my time there, and I entered it with a wide-eyed mindset and a sense of expectation.

High school was not hell for me, nor was it heaven. It was just there. I guess you might say that with all the build up, I was a little disappointed.

I started out the way I always knew I would: Go out for the football team and try not to be intimidated by all of the new people. I was living in the Ranchos and had been out there for four years—at the time, an eternity—and the schools I had been attending were filled with other kids like me, whose families had moved out there recently. We were all transplanted and going to schools full of transplanted kids just like us, but going to the high school in the actual city of Madera was totally different. There were a few kids from out in the Ranchos, but a ton from the city, not to mention that the high school was about ten times as big as the little schools I had been going to. My graduating class alone was seven or eight hundred kids strong, and each graduating class that followed grew in size. I had a couple of friends going in, but we all mostly drifted off into different worlds in high school—there were new options.

I was still friends with Gabe, but he was always hanging out with new people, and I was less adventurous. We started off high school like two scared children in the wilderness, and then we realized that no one was going to eat us alive. We had clashed plenty of times—junior high had been difficult, and he probably was the source of much of that difficulty—so we made other friends. We hung around with each other less and less, but yet somehow remained close throughout high school. We both joined the football team ... and we both quit after one practice. ("This sucks!") That was the end of Gabe's athletic career as far as I know. We were both tiny little guys as freshmen, but I wanted to do some kind of sport, mostly because that seemed normal and kind of fun—hey, you got to skip a class if you joined a

team, and when the season was over, you got a free period
... why not? I eventually found my way onto the water polo
and swim teams—the people were nicer, and the water was
cool in the summer. Worked for me.

I had no identity, I didn't know what I wanted to do or
who I really wanted to be, and I spent my first two years of
high school sort of drifting through classes and killing time.
I remember sitting in the offices of high school counselors
and knowing the whole time that I had no reason to be
there, and that the questions they were asking didn't apply
to me. It was that simple. I thought everything they were
suggesting, based on their little surveys and "personality
questionnaires," sounded the same, boring, and even then
I still had no idea what I wanted to do. I drew pictures
constantly, but had no desire to go to a school where I was
forced to draw pictures constantly, only to end up selling
paintings in malls and at sidewalk fairs. I just needed some
time, as most people do at that age, and that was all I knew
about my career—check the box marked "Undecided." I
wasn't part of any cliques or gangs or cults; I didn't even
hang with the water polo team all that much. They were all
older than me anyway. I didn't have any opinion on anything or care about any sort of style; I was just there. For
those first two years ... I was just there.

AND I DIDN'T EVEN HAVE A CAR

During my sophomore year, I went through all the
changes young people go through, but not just physically—I was also changing in my heart and my head. I was less
and less interested in the activities of the kids around me,
but I also started to realize that there were other activities
that could occupy my time. One of my uncles took me to a
concert by a guy named Larry Norman, who was a Christian who played the kind of music my dad had raised us all
on, and I had a great time. He was hilarious, and his songs

spoke to me ... it was strange, and something I hadn't expected. I found myself trying to remember the songs in my head that night after the show. Up until then I had heard a handful of other "Christian Contemporary" artists, as they were known then, and I thought they were all okay, but none of them really connected with me. Larry Norman did. I bought an album of his, *Only Visiting This Planet*, shortly after the concert, and spent hours trying to decipher the lyrics and their meanings. I was now officially a music fan.

I'd say that right around this time was the real beginning of what would become my strange relationship with music. I had listened to it before, but no more than your average kid. The difference though, was that I started to feel the music, not just listen to it. Unfortunately, my parents saw music, and the subculture that surrounds the music that young people listen to, as part of the gateway to a life of sin. I have always believed that a lot of that came from their generation and the focus that generation put on music and the subculture surrounding it. They would not allow us to listen to "secular" music—music that wasn't made by Christians—in their house, and no discussion was invited. As a result of them becoming "the kind of conservatives that former hell-raisers become," all music was initially viewed with a suspicious eye. (When I was in the seventh grade, my mother found a copy of Journey's album, *Escape*, in my bedroom. I was grounded for a week. Yes, that's right, Journey.) Of course, now I can see that they weren't really being unreasonable —they were just doing what they could to control the flow of bad influences on us. Back then it seemed like such an injustice. They tried to steer me away from it, but it just felt like part of life, and a reason that life could keep my interest. Despite their best efforts, I completely fell in love with music, songs, and melodies that I could sing in my room. I started to feel that I was part of the music I was listening to, and I thought to myself: "I know I could do that."

In the meantime, I was slowly being drawn back to my faith and spent more and more time with Cary, the youth leader I mentioned. At the same time, I grew more and more unsatisfied with the person I was. It wasn't that I was out drinking all of the time at parties or hanging out with girls and getting into trouble—although I do seem to remember one incident involving a Taco Bell parking lot, a convertible, and throwing up into something that reminded me of the bushes at my old house in Fresno—I just didn't like my constantly changing behavior. I would curse like a sailor at school and then clean it up wonderfully at home. I never thought of God at school or throughout the day, but then at home I would pray and read my Bible. I think God had been awakening in me the desire to be one person, all of the time.

Around this time, Gabe had been hanging around a bunch of kids from a big church group in Madera, and one night he invited me to a Bible study at a church called Grace Community. Of course, my parents let me go, it was probably a dream come true for them, but I just wanted to go because I really had no one to hang out with, and since my one friend was going, maybe I would have some fun. I didn't go in response to some audible call by God; I just went. Plus there were girls there ...

This was my first introduction to "Youth Group," and as a person in high school, it seemed safe enough. I would learn to really despise that whole scene later, but at the time, I saw no harm or wrong in it—just like everyone else. There were processes I could easily identify and, therefore, felt comfortable around. It was obvious who had been there longer than others, who were the popular kids, who was the favorite leader, etc. In other words, it was just like high school, only the people asked you to come. I felt welcome mostly; sure, there were some awkward interactions, but that was to be expected. I met a lot of people there who went to my high school, and even though I didn't really hang out with most of them at school, we would say hello when we passed in the halls or had classes together. The people there who I did get to know were probably the greatest benefit of the group.

Did I have any great experiences at Grace? Yes. Did I learn anything? Not really. Well, I learned how to look like a good Christian, even though I wasn't dedicated to following God's Word. I learned how to joke with other young people in a way that was acceptable to the Christians around us, and yet still feel like I was getting away with something sort of controversial. (Do all youth group leaders joke about bodily functions and the "crazy" stuff they did on their wedding nights?) Most everything else that they were teaching I had pretty much already heard; I just looked forward to the activities and was glad to keep going if it meant not being stuck at home on a Wednesday night. Many of the kids who went to the group were also learning about music and were just starting to care about bands and songs, and for once, I felt like I fit in somewhere.

During that year, I had a typing class, and one of the guys who went to the youth group at Grace was in the class with me. We were chatting at the end of class one day about some of the music we'd heard at youth group, and I was telling him about some of the bands I liked. He then asked me if I had ever heard of a band called U2. I hadn't, and so he loaned me a copy of the album *WAR*. I told him that I couldn't listen to anything that "wasn't Christian," but he told me not to worry, that they were Christians, so I took the album home. That night, U2 became my first and only favorite group, ever. When my mother asked about the spirituality of the band, I pointed out a part in the song "Sunday Bloody Sunday," where Bono says, "Claim the victory, Jesus won." Ahhh. Safe. I had no idea what he was talking about, but he said "Jesus won," and that was good enough. Of course, my thinking was totally flawed regarding my assessment of a band's spirituality, but at the time, I didn't care; I just wanted something to listen to, and I had worked out the technicalities. (My weird relationship with faith and music might have started there. I drew more and more conclusions about Bono, a man I have never known, and his faith as the years went by, based on magazine articles, photo shoots, rumors, etc. And don't think for a second that Bono's time of apparently wrestling with his faith didn't put me through all sorts of agony. I was always afraid he "wasn't Christian anymore." I didn't even know anything about him personally, but I sure did make a lot of decisions for him throughout the years.) This way of thinking would take an ironic twist much later in my life.

I got to know more and more of the group, and I started to hang around with them at school. One of the kids I saw all of the time was a guy named Jim. He was a big part of the group, and everybody knew him. Because he was a senior and I was still a sophomore, we weren't exactly close friends at first. But I could tell by the words he chose and the lack of gaudy, emotive language that had become standard at group prayer time, that he really meant it when he prayed, and I trusted his sincerity. One day during our lunch break at school, Jim was sitting on one of the benches at "the Mall," and I sat down next to him and all of his friends. There was some discussion going on about music, and I heard Jim and some of the other guys talking about a band. I listened in and realized that they were in the band, and making their own music. It had never occurred to me that someone my age could actually be in a band or make songs.

Cool. Again, I said to myself: "I could do that."

I admired them from a short distance, for a short time.

THE MOUNTAIN TOP

That summer, I went to my first Christian Summer Camp, and rededicated my life to Christ—meaning I had lost sight of my original intentions—and wanted to refocus and start over.

There's a term that people use when, after leaving home and going up to the mountains with a bunch of Christian people and constant daily reminders of Jesus and Christianity, that someone makes an emotional decision to "get right with God." It's called a "mountaintop experience." It's so easy to have emotional experiences at places like intense Christian camps and weekend "retreats," away from the cares and the temptations of everyday life, surrounded by God's creation and a twenty-four hour intravenous feeding of Christian propaganda. Unfortunately, many kids who become Christians in this setting don't last long in their commitment after the camp is over. Once they get back home, the reality of the cost of turning their backs on the lives they've always known hits them. By then, their emotions have settled back down, and they forget why they felt the way they did.

I did not have a mountaintop experience. I believe that God had been ... whispering into my subconscious—some Christians call this "God speaking to them" and I don't think they are far off. I believe He was letting me know He wanted me to live a life that would put to rest a lot of the conflict that had been eating away at me. When I came forward at the service that ended the camp, I meant it. My faith would take some turns in the next few years, but even through the hard parts and the bad times, the foundation was there.

Ironically, amidst all of the emotion that tends to be close to the surface near the end of a camp, the person who had invited me to start hanging with these Christian people,

Gabe, was the only person who didn't come forward at the big service. He sat, alone, surrounded by chairs, watching. Gabe had been hanging with these people, but he was slowly going his own way. And in yet another twist of irony, I think he was one of the few people there with any real love for truth, because he knew there would be talk about him and his lack of participation in what everyone else was doing. Every student who attended the camp came forward but Gabe. He remained consistent to his own heart, despite the outcome. (A good three-quarters of those who came forward at that big service completely forsook any association with God by the start of the next school year.)

Gabe had already told me he was not a Christian anymore, but I was really hoping that he would have a change of heart. He did not, and from that point on, he truly began the process of withdrawing himself from a friendship with me. I prayed for him, I cried in front of him, pleading with him to reconsider, because I was certain that he would die in his sins and go to hell. (Something Christian kids desperately fear might happen at any moment to someone they love who hasn't "accepted Jesus in their heart.") Gabe was not interested, and had simply decided that he no longer believed in God. This was my first experience with something like this. I think at one point I actually said to him, "You can't just stop being a Christian!"

But he had, and so Gabe basically faded from my life. We saw each other from time to time, but I just couldn't relate to him anymore. He would leave his house in the Ranchos and stay in Fresno for weeks. Sometimes he would call me when he was home; sometimes I had no idea where he was. He became more and more involved in the drug culture of the Fresno punk scene, with acid, ecstasy, and whatever pills anyone could get their hands on, and I just couldn't understand it. I think I feared it mostly, so I stayed away. By the end of high school, we hardly knew each other, and after it, I saw him a total of about five or six times before he disappeared entirely. I last talked to Gabe about six years after we graduated; he was married (to the same ex-girl-friend I mentioned earlier!) and had a child. I have no idea what he's up to these days, hopefully something better. Who knows ... maybe the seeds of who Christ is that were planted years ago finally found some light and some water. I hope.

SUMMER EDUCATION

The start of my junior year in high school would see a completely different Mark. I had given my life back to God, and had also discovered a new side to music that changed my life forever, Punk Rock. I had listened to a couple bands when Gabe and I were still hanging around all of the time, but they were the bands that everyone had heard of, and they didn't do much for me. The Sex Pistols were just kind of boring; the Dead Kennedy's were all right, but mostly because I loved the one song where Jello Biafra didn't sound so weird, "Holiday in Cambodia"; everybody knew that Suicidal Tendencies were the baddest, most rebellious band on the planet, but there was no way I could ever sneak that stuff past my parents without alarms going off all over the house; Social Distortion was also popular, but their songs weren't fast enough for me, so they didn't blow me away either. But there were two bands I fell in love with the first time I heard them: Minor Threat and Youth Brigade. Toward the end of our time hanging out together, Gabe and I had watched the greatest punk rock tour film ever, *Another State of Mind*, about a million times. The film was basically Youth Brigade and Social Distortion touring together across the country and barely surviving ("They paid us in rolllls of pennies. Rolllls of pennies!"), and it was great. The best part was the stop in D.C. where they stayed at a place called the Discord House, and this band that no one at the time had ever played for me, Minor Threat, played a show without microphones—and the whole crowd sang the songs loud enough to hear over the music. Right then and there, I was hooked on the energy, and once again I said to myself: "I could do that."

The summer before school started, a kid moved into a house down the street from me—essentially the house, there still weren't many out in the country at that time— and he had about a million punk rock records. His name was Todd Thomas, he was a semi-pro skateboarder from Utah, and along with more punk records than I had ever seen, he had every Minor Threat release in existence. (He also had more information than I wanted: Minor Threat had been broken up for two years. Tragedy. "Yeah, but if you listen to the lyrics of Salad Days, it makes more sense, man.") Not to mention pictures and posters of them and a ton of other groups. I learned about one band that would also become a permanent favorite, Bad Brains—to this day, I still listen to *Rock For Light* whenever I need to unwind. How could you beat four guys with dreadlocks flying all over the stage, or their lead singer doing back flips off of the drum riser?

I saw pictures of punks all over the world, skinheads who were Neo-Nazis and ones who were very much not, punks who took over entire towns in Europe ... my mind was spinning. The unstoppable energy was the first thing to grab me, but the sheer guts of it all made me love it.

Don't have enough money to hang out with the rich kids who look at your clothes like they're not good enough? Fine—go buy plaid pants at the thrift store, peg them until you can barely move, get some big black boots, and then go stand next to them until they are so uncomfortable they just have to leave! No girls want you to call them because they're too busy trying to get the quarterback of the varsity team's attention? Great! Shave off all of your hair, paint something ugly on your jacket, and then go sit next to her at lunch and give her your phone number! What difference does is make if she throws it away? She would have anyhow ...

This was for me. I became a Christian and fell in love with Punk Rock, all in a three-month span, and in one way or another, I have always felt most comfortable as that person.

KIDS IN GOD'S BLESSINGS

Right after school started, the band Jim was in was looking for a new singer. I had been hanging around with the group from Grace a lot, and Jim's band was made up of some of the kids who went to the study. I had drawn a couple of designs for them before they had any T-shirts—drawing on Levi's jackets or painting on leather jackets, just like I had seen in all of those magazines and on those record covers—and we had all become fairly good friends. Jim told me they needed a new singer, and he wanted to know if I wanted to try out. I tried to play it cool ... but oh yeah, of course I did.

This is about where the conflict that has floated around in the back of my mind for so long originated. I was invited to try out for Jim's band, K.G.B. (The name didn't have a meaning at first, they just liked that it was made of initials, like the mighty G.B.H. Oh well, what are you gonna do?) I wanted to make sure all bases were covered. After school, when Cary came over for discipling, I brought it up to him. He was sort of amused, and in a way seemed ... disappointed. He said, "Mark, it's not that big of a deal. I mean, every kid wants to be in a band. I mean, really, why do you want to sing in a band?" In a way I felt like I was in trouble or something. I felt guilty for wanting to join the band, fearing some prideful motivation. My parents were skeptical; they didn't want me to get all wrapped up in the idea that I might become some rock star or something.

I decided to pray about it. I had already begun to feel guilty of something that I wasn't—unless by someone implying that I might be made it true. At the same time, I was so excited about something I thought I could be good at popping right into my lap right at the time I was discovering it. It seemed like fate. Like a plan that was unfolding right in front of me. So, I told God, "Okay, if You want me to do this ...You'll make it happen." It was an innocent prayer, and totally sincere. I believed then that God answered it, and I still believe it today, but it hasn't been easy.

The conflict began the moment I started second-guessing myself. You can pray all day long, but if you start to look for sinful motivation behind every move you make, you will find it. I was at peace; I was excited in a completely innocent way. Then, people I respected, maybe too much, got me turned around.

Ever since then, a question blows through my mind whenever anything goes wrong, "Are you really doing what you are supposed to be doing?"

The van breaks down—"Is God trying to tell me something?" The show is a disaster—"What is God saying through this?" Didn't get the huge deal I was hoping for— "God must be trying to say ..."

It never ends. And why? Because right at the start, I let the words of others have more power to me than the still small voice of God. (If those questions were to plague me when everything was going fine, perhaps my answers to them would be different.) The truth is, life is full of trials and tribulations. I know now that not everything works out the way we plan it; I just needed half of my life to find that out.

There is a huge difference between humility and doubt.

I was humble for about ten minutes, and I've been fighting doubt ever since.

———————⊛———————

I came over to the bass player's house, where the band practiced, and I tried out. I was horrible. I had listened to a demo they made with the old singer, memorized his lyrics and just tried my best to sing like him, which is never a good idea. The guitar player, Greg, didn't speak to me once the entire time I was there. The bass player, Kirk, was polite, but he was older than me, like Jim, and I didn't really know him. I felt awkward. I just focused my attention on some of the potted plants in the living room of Kirk's house, and tried not to screw up.

I screamed my little brains out, and somehow got the gig.

I was so excited that I couldn't sleep that night, thinking about what it would be like to make a demo tape, or even a record, with our own songs. I thought about what it would be like to play a concert in front of people I didn't know, and with bands that I listened to. It was perfect for me, a kid with a lot of spare time and a creative mind. I stopped admiring them from a distance and joined the band. I felt God had answered my prayer—sadly, the fact it had been the answer I was hoping for somehow undermined a lot of my excitement, but I managed to make it through all right ...

We decided that we should probably have words for the initials making up our name, because the first question people always asked was: What does K.G.B. stand for? We decided that we needed to glorify God in everything we did—a thought that at the time was innocent of the trappings it may have collected years later—and that included our name. We also didn't want anyone to think that we were ashamed of our faith, so we decided that the words would be: Kids in God's Blessings. Ouch. Well, it

CHAPTER THREE

was a name at least ... just not for long. We hated the idea of calling ourselves "kids," because that wouldn't apply in the years and years that were surely to come of us playing music and releasing albums. (Hey, it's called ambition.) We played with what seemed to be a hundred different ideas for names, all inspired by the bands we were all now listening to and the faith we shared: Directed Youth, the Edict, Disciples, Voice of Compassion ... anything that would look good on a leather jacket.

One day after school, while at Jim's house—where we would eventually practice permanently—we were talking about the name issue, and Jim said, "Man, it's no big deal. There are so many different names we could have, Disciples, the Crucified—"

"Dude. That's it, that's our name ... The Crucified."

We loved how mean it sounded, and truthfully, how punk rock it sounded. We tagged Galatians 2:20 at the end of the name whenever we wrote it, so that any uptight Christian person who got bent out of shape would see the reference to the verse, "For I have been crucified with Christ, therefore I no longer live, but Christ lives in me ..." (Actually 2:19 and 20, but that was too much to write after a name on a sticker ...) We started calling ourselves the Crucified, and shortly after, booked our first show. And so it began.

S.E., CIGARETTES, AND ACCEPTABLE BEHAVIOR

The Crucified played its first show ever at Grace Community Church of Madera. We promoted the show as best as we knew how at the time, which was to put out flyers at the high school, and at a couple punk shows in Fresno. I remember being really nervous handing out flyers, afraid that people wouldn't even take us seriously, or that they just wouldn't want to come at all because we were Christians. There was also a show in Fresno on the same night as ours, the legendary band .45 Grave was playing, and we figured that show would take people from Madera away from us, especially since we were playing at a church. One kid at my school who I gave a flyer to, a guy named Paul, looked it over once quickly and handed the flyer back to me. He said, "No thanks. I'm going to a real punk show on Saturday—.45 Grave is playing in Fresno." I was embarrassed, but at the same time, I figured that anyone who didn't come to our show was just not coming because they were afraid of God or something—typical of the presumptuous behavior that I didn't realize I was exemplifying. Saturday came, and I was ready.

I had invited my friend, Todd, the one with all of the records, to come to the show with me.

He was a really strange guy with an extremely random sense of humor. He was loud and mischievous, but always in a way that made the people around him laugh. When he would skate at local ramps, he was always good for one or two very bizarre, usually very coarse outbursts. "MARK IS HERE, AND HE WILL NOW TELL US ABOUT JESUS CHRIST! WHY DON'T YOU ADMIT THAT YOU JUST WANNA POKE CHICKS LIKE THE REST OF US?!!! Tell us, Mark, do you POKE?!!" While pulling airs and vertical tricks that no one in Madera had ever even tried. He was not only into all of the cool bands, but he was also my first encounter with someone who claimed to be "Straight Edge." He had no problem talking to me about my faith, but I think he always watched me for inconsistencies, ready to point out that I was no different than he was. He would tease me about lumping him in with "all them SINNERS." Todd was totally faithful to what was then the Straight Edge creed, allegedly started by a group called SSD, but made famous by Minor Threat, in their song "Out of Step":

I don't smoke!
I don't drink!
I don't f---!
At least I can ... f------ think!

Todd used to sing these lyrics over and over like some
mantra for clean living. He would draw huge black Xs on
the tops of his hands with permanent markers—a mark that
clubs selling alcohol commonly used to signify the underage people—this was a common badge of honor for the
Straight Edge crowd. He used to tell me that if he could
keep himself from behavior that would control him, then
he must not need God, and more so, that I was being con-
trolled by God and Christianity rather than just handling
life myself. Without getting into all of the ways that Todd
sort of blurred the lines of his adherence to the Straight
Edge creed (Todd was also my first high school friend to
not only admit to, but also offer unrequested information
about his sexual relationship with his girlfriend. "Yeah ... no
thanks, Todd. I'll pass on the recap"), what burned me the
most about him and his Straight Edge ramblings was that he
seriously forced me to admit that I was afraid of the all of
the vices I had been warned about. I had assumed everyone
would struggle with the same things I was told I would
struggle with: sex, drugs, and of course rock 'n' roll. His
presence, and consistency (at least at the time), forced me to
admit that while God had saved my parents and me from
our sins and hell, there were plenty of people in the world
who weren't living out stereotypical lives of debauchery.
Had I gone down the road my parents warned me against,
I couldn't say that I would be doing as well as he was. Todd
was messing up my comfort level in what was a growing
mindset of self-righteousness, and I didn't appreciate it—it
made me doubt the exclusivity of virtuous living that I had
always believed belonged to Christianity.

Todd came with me to the show, and my mother dropped

us off. She and my father had attended the one and only "concert" that K.G.B. had put on—a painful thirty minutes of us standing on the floor in the office of the Madera County Farming Bureau, out in the middle of nowhere, surrounded by our parents and kids from our study—and it had been so bad I think she just couldn't take another night like it. Todd and I went into the church, the concert would be held in the high school youth group rec room, and Todd went wandering around the place while I got together with the guys and set up for the show.

We got ready to go onstage, which was the only part of the show I had prepared myself for. I had no idea what to expect after the music started.

Two strange things happened: First, a lot of people showed up. There were kids from youth group, family and friends, a lot of kids from around town, most of the punks from school, and even some I had never seen before in my life. And second, the pastor showed up—livid and absolutely freaking out.

Now, I had just been going to that church for Bible study, nothing else, so I didn't know many people on the actual church staff, or even what the pastor of the church looked like. I didn't know the difference between Liberal and Conservative Christianity yet, or that there were some churches that were just generally more uptight than others. I heard people whispering that the pastor of the church had shown up, and that he was really bent out of shape. Reason? Well, aside from the initial shock of there actually being kids at the church that were part of this new "punker thing," there were "non-Christians" everywhere, and some of them were outside the church ... smoking. "What are these people doing here?!! This is a church for heaven's sake!" I heard total shock and disgust, "Well, some things are just not acceptable on these grounds!"

I didn't even get it; I had no idea what was happening. I

CHAPTER THREE

was so shocked by the turnout and the fact that I had no idea what I was supposed to do as the singer in a band, that everything went completely out of control before I even realized it was headed that way. The youth pastor—a guy named Bob, who led our study group and was familiar with most of the kids, and was therefore a little more relaxed—tried to calm down the head pastor, and had succeeded until... the proverbial "other shoe" dropped.

Todd.

I hadn't seen Todd since the beginning of the night when we first got to the church. I never even thought to look for him with everything that was going on. But the pastor found him ... scribbling "graffiti" on the inside door of a closet! Oh, the horror! The so-called "graffiti" was actually about a quarter of an inch high, and consisted of two letters, with periods like little Xs:

S_xE_x

Straight Edge.

The show was over immediately. Everyone out, now.

Of course this little episode didn't go over well with anyone. A lot of feelings got hurt, and a lot of suspicions were confirmed. The fact is, most kids don't expect to be treated with respect when they're dealing with pastors or churches. Maybe part of that isn't justified, but I know that part of it is. Sometimes sanctification—in this context, setting oneself apart from the world as devoted to Jesus—doesn't require a hammer and a blowtorch. In this situation, I believe tact would have accomplished more.

I brought this up in order to share some perspective. This was the path I took to a life in music, and these were some of the experiences that path took me through. Yes, the first show was a disappointment, but it served as a sad indication of how the Church of today often handles itself in exchanges with the very people it is attempting to reach out to, and in a way, it prepared me for the future. I look back now and see the same kind of people touring with the Crucified and Stavesacre I have encountered all across the country throughout the years. It was my first experience with a church that wasn't ready to accept the "dirty" parts of ministry. These might have been people who needed a little more than dusting off—maybe, maybe not—but that church wasn't ready, or willing, to do the work.

Hopefully a lot has changed over there in the years that have passed. Either way, I have since learned that in too many instances, there are nonbelievers perceived as safe, and those who are considered unsafe—a distinction I've found nowhere in the Bible. I'm responsible to reflect Jesus to whoever is put into my life, and I feel an equal responsibility to shield those same people against anyone who would distort that reflection. I'm human; I don't need any help making situations more difficult.

The Crucified went on, obviously, and we played lots of shows. We made some serious progress from a band that had its first show—at a church in a little town called Madera—canceled, to a band playing a reunion concert to three or four thousand people halfway across the country. I had a decent career of about eight years with them, from the age of fourteen to right around twenty-three, and I have much more to tell regarding it.

Thinking of that first show, I wish I could say everything has changed since then, but it just hasn't. Unfortunately, I've been a part of exposing fans of our music to people just like the ones from that first church, but these days I'm committed to not allowing myself to contribute to that sort of bad experience whenever I can help it. I won't be able to stop the whole world from misrepresenting the God I know, but in my own small way, I can at least do something.

CHAPTER THREE

FOUR

The HigH Price of 'Packer' Pride

On our first tour with the band Puller, Stavesacre played a show in a suburb of Columbus, Ohio, at a small community church. We were sitting with Puller in the "backstage" area—in this case, the church kitchen—at the table after eating dinner.

Everyone was in a good mood; full bellies and clean restrooms are always nice for that. Geoff Riley, Puller's drummer who is not a Christian, was cracking us all up as usual, with one of his unbelievable stories. (All of Geoff's stories were a little unbelievable, which was perfect for his sense of humor and personality, because the stories were usually true. They are too many to name here without getting off track, but let's just say ... parents of childhood friends who were seen regularly taking baths in large trash cans, full of water and bleach, out on the front lawn ... That should give you some perspective.) As we carried on, a church elder came through the door and stood by a refrigerator, off to one side of the room, seemingly to share in the conversation.

CHAPTER FOUR

Now, in a church, there are many different functions, because there are many different things that have to be addressed regarding the day-to-day and year-to-year happenings within such an organization, and so for every function that demands attention, there must be someone to answer that demand. Depending on the size of the church, often many tasks can be carried out by one person, or even a small group of volunteers, although sometimes there are just too many things to accomplish, and the church may go so far as to have an entire staff of individuals whose actual jobs—how they make their living—are to handle these duties. There is usually some order that everyone recognizes, and that system is often just for the sake of organization. These people are known as "deacons" or "elders," and they usually have been members of the church for some time. Sometimes they're paid, and sometimes they volunteer. Ideally, after much prayer to God, weighed with careful consideration of a person's life and biblical teaching, a church congregation—those people sitting in the seats who are members of the church—can make a safe decision as to whom among them would be the right person to take such a visible role in the church.

Whenever we've played at a church, we've usually been introduced to at least one elder who will be overseeing the show. This person will—sometimes—just make sure that we know he or she is there, which I don't mind at all; it shows that the church isn't just a building, but that the people who call it their "church home" actually care about what goes on there. In this case, the gentleman who was leaning on the refrigerator was that person, the caretaker of the church and church property.

We had met him earlier in the day, but he wasn't much for conversation. We'll call him a little "stand-offish," not a monster, but not someone who made us feel welcome. This did not surprise me much; most church elders we've encountered in these situations are a little apprehensive, so we're used to it—besides, with what I've heard from people about me, I would keep an eye on me, too.

The truth is, I think the whole church was a little more than leery of us from the beginning. The promoter of the show was "that guy"—the black sheep of the church body, a kid who was most likely already suspect in the eyes of most of the congregation. The body language of the people around was that of strained tolerance. It carried on and multiplied whenever we had to interact with people from the church instead of the promoter, and it began the moment we loaded our equipment into the place. (A thought: Isn't it strange that the so-called "black sheep" of the church are often the ones doing something? At least, something other than sitting back and evaluating what everyone else is doing?)

The elder came into the kitchen where we sat, leaned up against the refrigerator, and quietly listened to our conversation. His body language was that of a person who wanted to draw attention to himself by not taking part in what everyone around him was doing. Because he didn't say much at first, we all mostly ignored him. After a while, his lack of participation in the conversation became uncomfortable. I mean, how long was this guy going to stand there and stare at us?

Eventually, there was an awkward lull between comments, and then the elder, looking right at Geoff, asked, "Is that hat part of your stage costume?"

Geoff, a loyal Green Bay Packers fan, was wearing a Packers cap, showing his pride in the then one-year removed World Champs. Thinking the elder was going to give him some good old fashioned ribbing, Geoff asked, "Well that depends ... am I being asked this by a Bengal fan—"

Before he could continue, the man cut him off.

"Because you're wearing that hat in a House of God ...

CHAPTER FOUR

and you ought to show some respect."

Awkward silence, now charged with some hostility.

Geoff, clearly surprised and embarrassed, immediately took his hat off and apologized, saying, "Oh, I'm sorry. I didn't mean to offend you; I'm very sorry."

Not hearing him, the hostile elder, now gaining some steam, continued on, "And don't think I'm just some old fogie (?!) trying to ruin your fun. If I didn't want you here, there wouldn't be a concert tonight in the first place."

It wasn't difficult to detect the pure disgust in the tone of his voice, and judging by the looks on all of the guys' faces, we all had the same thought: "This guy is really ticked off." We all sort of stared at each other, shocked; no one said anything for a few beats, and then the guy left. Geoff, not on his own ground, was totally sincere in his apology. He had no idea wearing this cap would be so offensive—who would? He just kept looking from face to face, as if to ask, "What'd I do?"

In the room that night, something started to die for me. I think it would be safe to assume the same for most of the guys there as well. I could actually feel the blister that had shown up on my heart in the last couple of years turning into a callous. Here we go again.

The whole scene was just unnecessary. I don't want to get into a Bible study on 1 Corinthians 11; there's not enough time. Let's just say that even aside from any debate regarding context, we are not instructed to embarrass each other in the place of rebuke—needed or not—ever. If this elder had a real problem with Geoff, and had his intention truly been to see a "house of God" respected, could he really justify rebuking a person he obviously assumed was a Christian— and therefore, a person who would even care about such a thing in the first place—in such a manner?

Just like every human being saved by the grace of God, I struggle to be more like Him and less like me, and I know that often I can lack attributes like gentleness, kindness, patience, long-suffering, and love—but this still doesn't make it all right for an elder in a church to act in such a way. These are the people we are taught to listen to, told to respect, and told will help to lead us "along the path." I guess the healthiest way to look at the situation is to use it as a reminder that only God is perfect, but does that mean that we accept this type of behavior and plow on through life?

Mike Lewis, the singer of Puller, was new to all of this, from the "Christian music scene" to Christianity itself, and I know he took it personally. It didn't just offend him, it hurt. Geoff was and still is one of his best friends. Mike had been trying to show Geoff a true picture of Jesus through his life and friendship, and I can only imagine what damage that picture had taken after such insensitive and petty bullying.

As much as it may seem naïve, there is, I think, still some part of us that holds people who are elders in the church—strangers or not—in a place of trust. Do these people realize that so many of us want them to be worthy of that? We want them to turn out to be ... good. Not perfect, just good. Do they realize how much of an encouragement this would be to us? To everyone? In this situation, an opportunity to display so many of the attributes of Jesus was lost, maybe permanently. You'd have thought by his tone of voice that he'd caught Geoff spray-painting "I Love Satan" (or ... S.E.!) on the front door.

Of course, Geoff, true to his non-Christian, super-pagan, evil-loving self, has always maintained that he can tell there is a difference between us and people like the deacon. Figures. The non-Christian shows the character.

CHAPTER FOUR

I felt bad for both Mike and Geoff and upset at this distorted display of Jesus "reaching out" to people. I know what was going on there: just one more case of one more person with the same old and tired preconceived ideas regarding what was "acceptable behavior for good Christian-folk." Just one more person who assumed too much of a situation that he really knew nothing about, but never the less proceeded. Was this normal behavior for him? How much can you learn about a total stranger in just a few short minutes?

Still, I can't help but think of what I know is true even in such a gross situation: "Judge not, lest you be judged by the measure with which you judge another." Am I, calloused heart and all, also guilty of the same callous-causing actions? What is my duty in this situation? To stand up and step into my stone throwing? Or is there something more that I'm missing? I have to admit that sometimes it's harder to see the truth. What would the correct response have been? Am I even capable of levelheaded thinking in such an awkward situation? Truth is, in these situations, I just want blood. It is so easy to sit back now and burn up the straw men of bad church related experiences, but what good is it? Even writing now, completely separated from the tension of those experiences, I feel like I just want to let it all blow away. Let the sleeping dogs lie, etc.

On the flipside of that, I have to remind myself that that is exactly the behavior that has allowed this sort of thing to go on for as long as it has, relatively unchecked. Hoping all of it goes away seems irresponsible. But as I write, I feel like I am learning something else, something higher, something more. Yes, I am very angry, yes, I want to actively change the problems I see, but I want to temper my anger and zeal with focus, reason, and solution.

Later on that night, Mike stood outside bouncing a basketball over and over against a shed. He was not to be consoled.

"People."

Bounce, bounce.

"You know, people have no respect."

I think of that night often, and I ask this question: What does God care about? I have a good idea of what most Christian people care about, but what does God care about?

I've seen in dark places
small flames cutting through where there were none
before
so simple, so precious
but still small, still open, still vulnerable
and this home sweet home
this shelter from the ever-present enemy
has kept score, and closed doors
brightest fires safe inside, close and comfortable
from the failures
and something's dying down inside of me
is this feeling? is this real?
well it must be something,
from nothing, nothing comes

"AN ECLIPSING"
Stavesacre, *Absolutes*

CHAPTER FOUR

I watch you bend beneath the weight
and it seems heavier these days
each time I see you force a smile
my heart just breaks
as I watch you bend beneath the weight
I don't believe this is what God ever intended
I think it's time to go
The sun is going down,
I say we follow it out of town
we've been here for far too long
(but will they know we're gone?)
In the morning when it rises
maybe it will shine for us ...
I want you to look me in the eye
and tell me if we stay here we won't die
they'll say we love the darkness
but I say we hate their half-light
and I wanted you to know
The sun is going down ...

"SUNDOWN MOTEL"
Stavesacre, *Speakeasy*

SIMPLICITY

THE CRUCIFIED —(Mark Salomon, Jim Chaffin, Jeff Ballew, Greg Minier)

FIVE

WHERE IT CAME TOGETHER

Maybe a year after the Crucified almost played their first
show, I met a person through a Christian music publica-
tion called *Christian Activities Calendar*. This guy had put
out an advertisement for himself, inviting any punks who
were Christians to call him up for information about other
punks. The number he gave for a contact was his home
phone. Of course, I called him that day.

Now, we already had all of the so-called "Christian Punk"
that was out there, but to be honest, it was seriously lacking. I mean, there was Undercover, who were playing songs
called "Jesus Girl" and "God Rules!" They were ... what
they were, but if you put that stuff on at the skate ramp,
you were gonna go home crying. There were also the Altar
Boys. They were a little rougher and a little more raw, but
still not nearly mean enough to freak out your parents. That
wasn't going to work either, and I still wouldn't play them
for my friends—they just didn't have the sound that my
friends and I listened to. But everything changed when I
picked up a phone and called the guy advertising himself

only as "Burrito."

I talked to Burrito for about three hours that day. He was all the way down in Los Angeles, but I couldn't get off the phone. I had no idea people like him even existed, and he knew of even more people like himself. He also had something about him that spoke of integrity and energy, not to mention that he had an infectious sense of humor, which was both foul and innocent at the same time. (Don't ask me, if you know him, it makes sense ...) I talked to him about all of the bands that he had seen down in L.A. and about all of the tapes that he could get to me, so I could hear all of these Christian punk rock bands. I got off the phone and could barely sleep that night, in anticipation of the coming mail ... which eventually showed up after I checked the mailbox every day for a week.

I got an envelope with a letter from Burrito, a list of about ten other bands from down there, and an address for an actual "zine"—short for fanzine or magazine—that was called *Zine of the Times*. It was the one legitimate Christian fanzine in those days that you could actually hope to get once you ordered it. It had pictures of bands I had never heard of and live photos from punk shows, as well as music reviews. On the list, there were bands with names like A.O.T.C. (Association of the Cross), Conviction of Sin, and Scaterd Few (sic). They were bands that actually sounded like punk bands I would listen to. There were phone numbers and contact info for all of them. Jackpot.

I contacted most of the people on the list, and I ordered demos from all of the bands that I could, but after weeks of listening to poorly recorded crap, I started to lose hope. Most of the bands turned out to be either broken up or just the same bands but with different names, and of course, some of them just weren't any good.

The last band left for me to try was down in San Diego, south of L.A., and they were somehow separate from the network of interchangeable bands. The band had previously been called Pontius Pilate and the Pious Punks but was now called Point Blank, and the kid whose contact information was listed on the sheet was named Bill Power. Once I got ahold of Bill, he sent me a whole fat envelope full of flyers and pictures, as well as a cassette demo of his band. They were actually good, and I was in shock. We immediately asked Bill and his band to come up to Fresno and play with us for the Crucified's actual first show.

HOW TO START OUT
BY PAINTING YOURSELF INTO A CORNER

I was in the Crucified for about two years before we played that first show. We practiced about three times a week (high school kids tend to have a lot of spare time), but it took us two years to actually get a real show together. We didn't really try, and we also knew we weren't ready. We would go over to Jim's—first practicing in his bedroom, then in the garage, where we remained for about four years—every day after school. Once we finally felt that we had strong enough songs to play in front of other people, we made a demo tape at a local studio, tracking something like fifteen songs in two days. We called the demo *Take Up Your Cross* (and thought we were so original). Burrito had me send him our demo, which he then duplicated on cassettes of old teaching tapes from Calvary Chapel of Costa Mesa, the parent church of the Calvary Chapel I went to in Fresno. (Burrito and I are still friends, and those tapes are one thing that gets brought up just about every time we get together ... typos and all: "Tack up your Cross" on the label and Raul Reese's voice still almost audible in between songs ...)

When Bill and his band got to our town, we were a full-fledged band, with music, band T-shirts, and decent equipment. It was a totally new experience for me, meeting a completely separate group of Christian musicians, and then welcoming them into our world. (Bill—like Burrito—is still very much a part of the music scene of today, playing a major role in developing Tooth & Nail Records, and making music in a few different bands. He is also one of the few people not related to me to have ever tasted my mother's pancakes …) We were able to spend time around Christians from entirely different backgrounds, which served as one of the first times I would be given the opportunity to realize that my Christian experience wasn't the only Christian experience. The show was a bit uncomfortable, with a lot of people sitting down or dyeing their hair pink that day, then showing up to the gig and feeling embarrassed and out of place. But, there were a lot of people there, including at least half of the Fresno punk scene—who spent the entire night standing off to one side of the hall, staring straight ahead at the band and not acknowledging anyone else in the room—and we felt like we had something that we could build on.

For the next few years, the Crucified rarely played, but we were totally serious about the band. I was slowly growing in my relationship to God, but I was also in uncharted territory with the band and with my faith. No one really knew what we were supposed to do. We felt that if we didn't make it clear that we were Christians with every opportunity to do so, we would be hiding our faith and letting God down. We were committed to preaching at every show, sometimes even having an altar call. We preached at shows because we thought that we should, and no one ever thought otherwise. We continued, despite all of the times that I would be preaching, and halfway through the message, lose track of where I was, or just spit out skewed and uninformed doctrine—all that mattered was that we preached. That was always the concern. Not necessarily what I said, as long as it wasn't heresy, but that I said something.

Throughout the duration of the Crucified's existence, we
preached at every show. This made sense to me, kind of, but
I never even considered that what I was doing would come
back to haunt me, years later, and long after all the damage
was done.

Some thoughts and memories of those early days: Everyone piling into Jim's Volkswagen Fastback; Greg's hair—
surely, one of the earliest sightings of the mullet; my ridiculous clothes—"Mark, did you really think that you could
paint on a brown leather jacket and have it look cool?";
Trevor, our second bass player, drawing cartoon caricatures
of us inside the lyric sheet to *Take Up Your Cross*, and us
laughing at it for so long that we decided to just put it in
the artwork we handed out to everyone who bought the
tape anyway. There were a lot of boring days spent doing
nothing but practicing and practicing, but I never felt like
I was wasting my time. I felt like we were building something.

It didn't take long to get bored trying to find interesting ways to put together the same three chords. We steadily
developed a desire for the most powerful music we could
find, and ways to create our own sound in the process. Greg
always loved heavy metal, which I hated, but Jim was sort
of in the middle. Trevor didn't really care; he just didn't
want us to suck. After a few years of listening to the same
albums over and over again, we started to explore. The first
hybrid form of punk rock and speed-metal we heard was a
band from the northern California city of Berkeley called
Corrupted Morals. I wouldn't call them a pioneering band,
but they were the first band we heard to really put down
the sound we were leaning toward, and we decided to just
keep going in that direction. The speed and energy of punk
combined with the heavy chords of metal made for some-

thing that satisfied everyone's tastes.

One night Greg played me *Ride the Lightning* by Metallica and changed my appreciation for metal guitar riffs. (Maybe not quite to the point where I was willing to overlook my hatred for it enough to completely cross over ... but I would at least listen to some of it willingly.) Jim started playing with a double-kick drum pedal, and it became a huge part of our music from then on. It wasn't gaudy like the double-bass drum setups bands such as Slayer used, but it still required the same skill and stamina. It gave the music just a little more speed, which at the time was all that mattered. And not long after that, somebody found a copy of *Speak English Or Die* by S.O.D., and we were content. It was the perfect blend of all the styles we loved, with a touch of insane and absurd humor. I had to admit it: "Okay. Some metal is cool."

We really didn't do much proactively, as far as playing outside of our area, for the first half of the Crucified's existence. There was school to think about, and all of the hassles that came with it. The world outside of Madera and Fresno was too big to think about, so for a while, we didn't.

FOUR AND OUT

High school passed quickly, and I wish that I could mention all of the great times from those years. (And wouldn't you be bored?) Friends came and went ...

Trevor quit the band shortly after high school ended because he was going to college. We replaced him with bass player number three, Mark Johnson, a short time later. He played in a group that we did a few shows with called Martyr from a neighboring San Joaquin Valley town called Porterville. They were basically a speed metal band, and Mark definitely had the look: His long straight hair would have fit right in with Metallica or Slayer. The truth was, he loved punk rock probably about as much as he loved metal.

Todd eventually got bored with Straight Edge, got into hip-hop, and moved away. I saw him years later, walking down the street in a bad Fresno neighborhood, so I picked him up. He had been living on stolen credit cards, was doing drugs—I never found out which ones and I never asked—and then later converted to the Nation of Islam, adopting not only their way of life, but also their style of speaking (short responses, low tones—not Todd ...) and their history ... something which was a bit confusing coming from a guy with blond hair and blue eyes. ("Man, I found out some stuff about me and my own history that you will not believe, Mr. Mark.") I saw him once or twice after that; then he just vanished.

I saw Gabe at some of my shows, but not until much later, and he was no longer the same guy I grew up with.

Aside from the girl that ended up with Gabe, I really only had one other girlfriend in high school. Her name was Therese, and she passed away during my senior year. Although we had been broken up for about six months, we were still fond of each other in the distant way kids are still capable of. Her passing gave me my first taste of the finality of death—the first I was old enough to understand, yet young enough to have a nearly impossible time believing. I would have dreams that she was walking across my front yard while she called out my name, or I would be at school, hanging out in the mall, and she would just walk up to me and say, "Hey, I'm back. I wasn't really gone." It was my first real tragedy, but I think that when people are young, they're able to bounce back much quicker from experiences that later in life tend to require a lot more time.

All the while, I just kept focusing on music, and I really believe that was healthy for me. There are so many different twists and tangles that can turn an average kid into a bad one—who can count all of them really?—but with music, I always had a release for exactly what was going on in my head. I knew I could always turn to songs, lyrics, and the friendship I shared with the guys in the band, in order to express—and release—the pressures that built up inside of me.

Jim started going to my church, and we all slowly stopped going to the Grace youth group—especially after the episode with the pastor—although I think we all just outgrew that sort of setting. The end of high school means the end of high school youth group ...

Life moved on, and we went with it.

TO ERR ON THE SIDE OF CAUTION

An interesting thing to me that I've noticed while thinking back on all of those early days was my comfort level with calling people "Christian Punks" and referring to bands as "Christian Bands"—something that I completely detest today. The labels back then meant nothing that they mean now ... that has changed, and not for the better. Back then, while there definitely was an assumed responsibility to make sure no one ever thought we were afraid to admit we were Christians, the whole Christian-"whatever" label held a much different connotation. It meant that you were part of a network of people who were in the minority, and who were just looking for others who held the same beliefs. When we decided to call our band "Kids in God's Blessings," we did so because we wanted to give God glory, not because we were trying to please other Christians.

There wasn't an entire industry devoted to producing, marketing, and distributing the music we were all making and trying to find more of, nor were there all of the trappings that come with that industry. Sure, without that industry, it was very difficult to get anything—I would wait for months before an album or tape I had ordered from some zine would come in the mail—but there also weren't all of the lame snares that came later on: subjective standards shared by kids and retail stores all over the country; publications that would immediately judge the worth of an album based on its "spiritual content"—something so arbitrary that it was impossible to live up to enough to please everyone; or the different tides of opinion on what every band should or should not do, coming in and out of the public mindset. The regular world (known by many Christian people as the "secular industry"—I prefer simply, the music industry) has people who review and judge bands and albums based on musical merit, performance, relevance, and sometimes-moral content. (Obviously, there is a whole other set of politics and unwritten, subjective laws in the general market world, but few in that world would claim it to be otherwise. An almost forgotten truth about the Christian market—in light of what it has become—is that at one point, it could claim a freedom from those politics. It claimed to be virtuous, while the general market was always assumed to be guilty for lacking anything virtuous or ethical.) The Christian industry has become sort of the opposite, all from the posture of "caring more" about what God must surely care about: "spiritual" (once again, subjectively defined) lyrical content; image in light of one's "witness"— ideally, how they represent the message of Jesus—which, depending on what Christian you're talking to, can be everything from the life you live, to the words you speak, and even to the clothes you wear or what you eat and drink. In that order, mostly.

Did you know that the Gospel Music Association—giver of Dove awards, the Christian industry's weak answer to the Grammys—at one point felt the need to make a standard with which they could judge whether or not a "Christian Artist" was Christian enough, that included how many times the band said "Jesus" in their lyrics? As if such a thing could determine spiritual health. And doesn't any of that border on token use of the name of our Savior? (Be ner-

vous.) The emphasis in this so-called Christian industry isn't
on the quality of the art being generated, but on the appearance of a quality of spirituality—something for which,
once again, the definition would differ, depending on who
was appraising that quality of spirituality. Ugh.

Not much has changed yet. While I think some great
bands have come around directly related to the growth of
this industry, I think the quality of the music, and ironically, the spirituality of the individuals within it, has suffered
as a whole. If you "tow the party line," no one gets upset.
Say the right things, even if they aren't true; wear the right
clothes, as long as they have the token reference to God;
play the right concerts because the money is good. The
alternative is just too much hassle, and could end up de-
stroying careers that have taken years and years to develop.
One false move—and not necessarily sin, just different from
whatever is ambiguously labeled "safe"—and a million parents across the country will not allow their children to buy
your album, shop at your store, or listen to your radio station. If only some of these parents and music buyers knew
all of what went on behind the scenes with some of these
artists and performers that they are so sure about—because
they have always said the right thing, played the right music,
and so on—entire bookstore chains would go out of business.

And what would be a very sad, very real reality of this
disaster? Some of the infractions that these artists or industry folk might be found "guilty" of are often not sin
at all! Welcome to legalism on a nationwide scale. And
what do we say to those who would lament such bondage? "Hey, you're in the public eye ... You have to be more
careful than the average person (me) ... You're a minister
(I think), so you will be judged more strictly ... You are a
role model, and therefore have more responsibility to not
be a stumbling block ..." and on and on. Meanwhile, catch

phrases and opinions of our subculture are upheld as Law, and context in Scripture is ignored. The true responsibility of the children of God is changed and manipulated in light of individual experience, rather than made to adhere to the hard-lined, unchanging Word of God.

So, appearances are maintained. But when you look deeper, especially at some of the general opinions shared within this subculture of musicians and music fans—in other words, most of the people I've ever met—you will find bondage, confusion, error, and incorrect thinking that runs so far back most of us have a hard time finding where it started.

All of this, mostly to succeed in not falling short of the extra-biblical standards that some Christians have assumed must be upheld in order to remain ... "godly," and therefore marketable, or, "acceptable for youth-related functions." It's like a shortcut to fellowship, a shortcut to community, and a shortcut to Christianity—all for the sake of keeping the labels intact that enable the industry to run with as little inconvenience as possible. All for the sake of erring on the side of caution. Our collective spirituality has suffered for the sake of appeasing church associations and major contributors, who are in turn attempting to appease the perceived desires of their congregations and those who might be associated with them, and on down the line. It has suffered because we don't know how to let each other just live, and grow—everyone has to be an example from the moment they step onto the stage, regardless of all of the unknown events, decisions, trials, or tragedies that may have led up to that moment in that person's life ...

So ... are we a success?

BIG CITIES, SMALL MINDS, HIGHER EDUCATION

I graduated high school and got a job. The Crucified continued to practice religiously, and we got to playing more and more shows. We also started to look further than Madera and Fresno. Burrito remained in contact with us. He hooked us up with a guy who ran a church in Orange County, just south of Los Angeles, who wanted to bring us down to play a show in Hollywood at a Christian club called the Oasis. We went down for our first road trip, all piled in a van, and headed for "the big city" with no idea what we were strolling into.

First of all, Hollywood was a shock. We had grown up as most people outside of L.A. do, seeing Hollywood in films as this glamorous place, hearing about the "Walk of Fame" and all of the stars on the sidewalks, anticipating all of the lights in the city. We arrived at the club, which was just off of Hollywood Boulevard on Cherokee, and climbed out of the van, then almost jumped right back in. The city was a filthy, vile gathering of waste in the streets, smog in the air, and crazy people tucked into every nook and cranny they could wedge themselves into. We pulled into a parking lot at the back of the club and parked next to a trash can full— I mean full—of porn, right next to the back door. When we got there, the club wasn't open, so we walked up and down Hollywood Boulevard and checked out the stores and shops. The so-called "Walk of Fame" was a sidewalk with giant stars that contained the names of former entertainers most of us had never heard of, littered with vomit, trash, feces, and cardboard boxes that many of the residents of Hollywood used as homes. We were obviously small town folks ... culture shock took over. We were so uncomfortable we felt we had to escape as soon as possible. The club opened, we played, and we split. None of us felt safe until we were back up north, on our side of the mountains that separate the L.A. basin from the San Joaquin Valley. And yet, after all of that, we understood that to "make it" in this business, we needed to make a name for ourselves down there, somehow.

I started junior college and spent most of my days after

school looking for more music and record stores. At that time, Tower Records was about the only corporate store you could find any punk rock (or its new little brother, hardcore)—which they put in their "independent" music section, mostly because only small independent labels and distributors carried any of it—aside from local independent record stores. One day, I stopped into a small store that sold new and used CDs, records, and tapes. The store specialized in two kinds of music: punk records and twelve-inch hip-hop singles for DJs. I met the owner, a guy named Paul Cruickshank, who, aside from owning the store, was also always trying to do something proactive for the scene in Fresno. He booked bands, put on shows, and eventually even put out music on his own label named after his store, Ragin' Records. I talked with him that first day and spent whatever cash I had in my pocket on a couple albums that he suggested. (By then I had learned how to keep the good music hidden from Mom and Dad ... hey, you gotta do what you gotta do ...) I spent my lunch break there the next day, and the next thing I knew, I was working at the store for a few hours a day while he ran errands. In return, he paid me a couple bucks a day and gave me first pick of all the music I wanted, wholesale. My record collection soon became much larger. I could no longer hide it behind my stereo; I had to move it to the closet. (Paul still loves to tell people that I walked into his store one day, asked if I could eat my lunch there, and never left. Hey, at least someone was in there ...)

For the first time, I was hearing more than D.C. bands. I listened to all the N.Y. hardcore stuff I could, a lot of which came out on a label called Revelation, although there were so many small labels popping up, they were hard to keep up with. I loved Youth of Today, Gorilla Biscuits, Agnostic Front, and the Cro-Mags. I was educated in Orange County and L.A. bands other than Social Distortion and

Youth Brigade (who lived in L.A. but "actually were from Canada!"), both old and new like Uniform Choice, the Adolescents, X, Bad Religion, Agent Orange, even the legendary Circle One or the Germs. There were also the more melodic bands that I, along with every other wannabe-tough-guy punk rocker, secretly loved: Dag Nasty, MIA, and 7 Seconds, among others. I gained an appreciation for bands that weren't punk bands, but had their own appeal, sometimes even becoming preferred over the usual two hundred beats-per-minute bands: the Cure, R.E.M., and Fishbone. There was also an odd group of bands Paul kept insisting I would like that came from a (then) new indie label up in Seattle called Sub Pop. They had a singles club, where you could sign up for club-only releases (which of course we sold in the store anyway ...) from rock bands—decidedly not heavy metal bands—with long hair and names like Mudhoney, Soundgarden, Green River, and yes, Nirvana. I actually held in my hand the Sub Pop 700 (I think ... who can remember all of those numbers?) Box Set, which contained a bunch of loose, album-size photos of the bands, and something like four or five twelve-inch LPs. I still remember holding the Holy Grail of all Sub Pop Singles Club releases: the Nirvana split with Sonic Youth. "Nirvana? What's with all of that hair? Pass."

With all of the new information I was gaining, I could sense an appreciation for music that wasn't all speed and blisters developing. A process started in my head, and I couldn't stop it: I was getting bored playing songs that all sounded the same. (Who wouldn't?) The Crucified was still fun, but as a result of broadening my tastes, I started looking for more to go on in our music than just punk anthems and speed metal drum beats. The problem was, as we became more comfortable playing live, we began to enjoy a solid reputation for shows full of those anthems and fast songs. This kept playing that style of music interesting, so I was appeased for a little while ... but just a little while.

We played a few shows in Fresno, but received more resistance from the local punk scene now that we were playing in their venues and on the bills with their bands. We were trying to find a place where we fit in, but it wasn't looking good. For instance, another local independent record store owner put out a seven-inch compilation record, called *Fresno Shreds*, and used past flyers from Fresno shows as the art work on the disc jacket. A San Francisco area band called Attitude Adjustment played a show that Paul put on at the Knights of Columbus Hall, where all of the Fresno shows happened. We played as well, and the flyer for the show had our name on it. When the *Fresno Shreds* compilation came out, that flyer was used for the artwork, but our name had been taken off of it, and another band's name had been put over ours. When we asked the guy later why he felt the need to change it, he flatly replied, "I just didn't think a Christian band had any business being on a punk rock compilation." Too bad; it would have been the closest thing to a seven-inch record we had ever had. (As a former record collector myself, that would have been nice to have.) Sure, it would have been cool to have been on the comp, but we didn't even think about that—we knew where we stood.

NOT SUCKING AS THE EXCEPTION, NOT THE RULE

We received a letter in the mail from a kid out in Chicago who had read about us in the zine Z.O.T.T., asking for our demo tape, *Take Up Your Cross*. His name was Chris White, and he actually sent the three dollars for the tape right along with his letter ... in CASH! We sent him the tape; I think by then we had recorded our second demo, *Nailed*, which we might have sent along to him as well. In his letter he said, "If your demo is the same crappy sounding kind of recording that just about all the other ones that

CHAPTER FIVE

I've gotten have been, could you please just send me my money back? I'm tired of buying demos that sound like they were recorded on somebody's stereo." After he listened to the music, studio quality as always, he wrote back and thanked us for basically ... not stealing from him.

In those days, finding people into the same music that we were into was still a rarity, and Chris and I started a correspondence. As it turned out, he actually did like the music, and he let me know that he and some friends had been listening to the tapes quite a bit. He also mentioned that he was part of a community of Christian people who all lived together in Chicago called "Jesus People USA." They published a monthly magazine called *Cornerstone*, and every year they organized a festival with the same name. He said that he would give our music to someone from the community named Spike who wrote for the magazine, to see if he would write a review.

Spike gave our demo a positive review, and the review started a small buzz—enough of a buzz to get us invited to play Cornerstone. We flew out and played our first Cornerstone the summer of '88.

The "fest" was great, although a lot more simple then than it is now. Also, it was a lot less cost-effective for Jesus People USA, usually referred to as JPUSA ("juh-pooz-uh"). They would fly the bands out, give them a hotel and food money the day they played, and then have a hospitality room set up at the hotel where the bands could snack and hang out all day, instead of being outside—in the sun, in the middle of summer, in rural Illinois—all day at the festival. They used to hold the festival at an actual fairgrounds, but everyone thought that was a drag—we played it two or three times on the old grounds, and let me tell you, with flat fields and nothing to do but listen to bands and walk around, everyone was right. Eventually, they moved to a former pig farm in Bushnell, Illinois, that JPUSA purchased and is still in the process of developing. And that's where it's held now. (The farm smells awful whenever it rains—usually in buckets—but at least there's a lake, trees for shade, and places to take a walk and get away from all of the music and people.) It was like a working holiday, and the free food and hotels made it really easy to show up for.

Understandably, they don't do much of that anymore—except the hospitality room and payment for playing—but it's still the single best show that most Christian bands play all year. Before the Cornerstone Festival, the biggest crowd we had ever played for was about three of four hundred people. Our first time ever playing Cornerstone, we played to about three thousand screaming, sweating, stage-diving, crowd-surfing kids who were absolutely ecstatic about the fact that they were hearing a Christian band playing music like ours. It was a great gig, and a big break for us. It also showed us what it might be like if our music took off in the rest of the world the way it did there.

Cornerstone is now a fixture on the Christian festival scene, and holds the reputation of having all of the bands that the kids are actually listening to on their festival itinerary. Those first years though, there were only two punk bands that played, the Crucified and the Lead ("leed," not "led"). It has grown so much now that a band doesn't really get a break just by playing the festival because there are too many other bands to compete with. However, the bands that truly are good get noticed even faster than they ever have, because the fans are so hungry for originality that when a band comes along that connects with them, word spreads fast. But in 1988, there weren't any other bands, so there wasn't much of a choice. I attribute that high demand and low supply to the perceived success and supposed size of the Crucified's fan base. (To this day, people still think of that band as having been highly successful and selling a lot of records ... when in fact, by the end of the Crucified, we

CHAPTER FIVE

had maybe sold about a third of the records Stavesacre sold in its first two years of existence, and played about a tenth of the shows—total—that Stavesacre had played after about two years of touring.)

ACCEPT JESUS! OR GO MEET HIM TODAY!

We were booked to play a show in southern California again, this time at a church in Anaheim called Set Free, which was home to a group intent on ministering to all of the punks and street kids in the Orange County area. The group was called Out-of-Step Ministries, a title taken from Minor Threat and their song called "Out of Step (With the World)." The logo on the flyers they sent us was a punk with a huge liberty-spiked mohawk, carrying a cross. A man named "Biker James" had contacted us and brought us down. He was a good guy, and it was obvious that he loved his community. The kids all sort of hung around him, and you could tell they were close; they knew his wife and his whole family. He was also the first Christian we'd met with tattoos from head to toe, and he seemed comfortable around people whose appearance usually caused such an uproar in the stuffy churches we were used to.

We made the trip down to the L.A. area once again and played to a packed building, full of punks, skinheads, and bikers, with a few heavy metal fans sprinkled in for good measure. It was great, our first real show in a completely different town, and we did well. We came down a couple more times for shows with James and "Out-of-Step," forming friendships and building relationships with other bands and people from the ministry.

The theology of the church James worked out of, Set Free, was probably the most difficult part of our initial time spent down there. I would say that throughout the years, the hardest interaction I've had with people all over the country has been with the many different theological views and church doctrines that I've found myself surrounded by. Caught away from familiar comforts, and in close quarters with people who carry themselves differently than I do, has always been difficult. Sometimes the nonessentials are so different that fellowship is almost impossible. Set Free was an extreme example of my point, as they were—and still are, judging by every encounter I have had with them since—doctrinally nowhere near where I stand. As a first real experience with that sort of strange awkwardness, Set Free was perfect, setting a tone that has remained a constant throughout my career. By the Crucified's second show at Set Free, James had apparently felt the same way, and was already on his way out. By the third show, he had completely disassociated himself with them.

There were strange comments made at that first show, including rhetoric about being "totally committed" and "trained to serve Jesus!" The impression was more of a bunch of ex-bikers starting a new motorcycle gang as an alternative to the Hell's Angels, only they would "Kick a-- for Jesus!" We didn't notice it as much that first time, but the second show, we noticed that things seemed a little off. James had booked the gig and then didn't come around, but no one at the church would say why. It seemed like they wouldn't say why for a reason, but we were still too new to the situation to know what was going on.

When we showed up for the third show, which Phil, the "pastor" of Set Free booked on his own, we were told that James was no longer affiliated with the church. We played the show, and then went backstage because "Pastor Phil" was going to deliver the message. As I walked to the backstage area, I noticed all of these huge bikers walking toward the doors, and then standing in front of them. A friend that was acting as our manager at the time, Wayne—the very same Wayne I read my first song to back in high school—needed to leave right after the show, so he came backstage with us, said goodbye, and then split. A few minutes later, he returned to the backstage area, red in the face and flustered.

"They won't let me leave!"

We all looked up at him and saw he wasn't kidding.

"What do you mean? They won't let you out the door?" we asked.

"No! They have these big biker guys standing in front of the doors, and the doors are locked! Some guy said to me, 'Hey! No one leaves while Pastor Phil is speaking!' I told them I had to go, that I was with the band, and they said they didn't care!"

We got Wayne out through a door in the backstage area. When it was safe, we loaded up our equipment and never played for Set Free again.

There was one good thing that did come from that show: We played with a band we had never heard of up until that point, but who had been playing in the area regularly and gaining a following. They were called Vengeance (later changing their name to Vengeance Rising for legal reasons) and they soon became close friends and show partners of ours. They were completely and totally committed to "the Metal." As far as I know, they were the first Christian band to play speed metal and put out a record. (They were also a part of a church nicknamed "Metal Church" for all of the longhaired heavy metal fans who attended it. A man named Bob Beeman led the church—a tall, older guy with this huge head of long curly hair that I have always suspected wasn't his own ... He was a decent person, and so were most of the people who attended the church, which was actually called Sanctuary. Vengeance was a major part of a whole movement within a crowd of former partiers who were now Christians. Many of them were getting saved and putting together Christian bands. In my opinion, Vengeance

was the best band of the lot.) When they took the stage, all
four of the guys up front—both guitarists, the bass player,
and the singer—spun their heads around like windmills, in
time with the music. Not my thing, but Greg and Jim (the
closet metal-head) were in heaven.

Once we got in touch with James again, he started booking shows for us regularly. He never really got into what
went down at Set Free, which I thought showed class, but
it didn't matter by this time: James had started his own
church, the New Vine. All of the kids who had been going
to Set Free had been there because of him anyway, so when
he started his own church, they followed him right on over.
James also started booking shows at a high school auditorium in the Orange County suburb of Garden Grove, at Lake
High Continuation School. We played there about once a
month for the next few years, gathering a following that
seemed to grow and grow, until we couldn't fit everyone
in the auditorium anymore. From there, we started getting
calls for shows all over Orange County and L.A., and their
respective surrounding counties, like Oxnard, Ventura, and
Riverside.

NARROWPATH

Around that time, I received a phone call from a man
named Greg Sostrum. He had heard of us and of the shows
we were playing, as well as the number of kids who were
showing up. He said he was starting a record label, and
wanted to know if we were interested in signing on. At the
time, I knew nothing about labels, marketing, distribution,
or even how much we were supposed to get paid. All I
knew was that a record label had just called my house, and
wanted to put out our album. I freaked out, called the guys,
and they freaked out—except Greg, who never freaked out
about anything—and we prayed about it. We felt that God
had brought this opportunity to us, and we all agreed that

as good stewards of His blessings, we should do it. I called
Greg Sostrum and told him we were into it. He sent the
contracts, and that was that.

The label was called Narrowpath Records, and they put
out the Crucified's first self-titled album. I believe God was
looking out for us, because with no lawyer or legal counsel,
we somehow avoided being completely robbed. The album
didn't sell much, and we never made any money, but we
did put out the first CD from any band in Fresno. (Which
was a nice touch of poetic justice for the guy who put out
the *Fresno Shreds* compilation. Not only did his band, a
great punk band called Capitol Punishment, not have any
music out on this "new" type of format—yes, the compact
disc—but we also were able to record the album at a legendary studio in Orange County called "the Casbah." The
studio was famous for albums from future punk rock icons
like Social Distortion and the Adolescents. I remember sitting on stacks of reels for albums like *Mommy's Little Monster*
and wondering if that guy still thought we had no business
in punk rock ...)

The Crucified's first album was full of songs we had been
playing for years, and some new ones that touched on styles
we had been gravitating towards. The artwork was fairly
simple, but the inside was supposed to contain the logo
that we would use for years to come—a cross made out of
three nails, with a crown of thorns behind it. This became
the Crucified's emblem. For all the logos I had designed for
other bands throughout the years, it was the first real piece
of my artwork to be seen in places other than my bedroom
or the back of a friend's jacket. Unfortunately, it only made
it onto the album by way of a photo: The back cover of the
album jacket had a picture of me jumping through the air,
with a tattoo of the emblem on my arm. The manufacturer
took a handful of pictures we laid out for the inner sleeve,
made a collage inside the album, and left out the lyrics and

emblem art we sent along. It was a slight disappointment for us, but no one really minded ... we had an album out. We were a real band.

"OH, HOW THINGS HAVE CHANGED"

We played a club on the Sunset Strip called Gazzarri's that we had seen once in a movie called *The Decline of Western Civilization: Part Two—the Metal Years.* We were over our fear of Hollywood and knew that if we were ever going to break, something that we probably couldn't even define at the time, we needed to play the clubs where all of the real record companies would see us. Narrowpath had mostly dwindled into nonexistence, and we didn't expect much to come of it, and neither did Greg Sostrum, who let us out of our deal and gave us his blessing to pursue something else.

We got to the club, loaded in, and went looking for some lunch on "the Strip." We ended up at a little sandwich shop with big windows that looked out onto Sunset Boulevard. As we ate our food, a group of young, tough-looking kids came walking up to the front of the restaurant—all of them were dressed in black sweatshirts with big red letters printed on the front—stopped in front of the window, looked in, right at us, and walked in through the front door.

Great. Everybody up in Fresno had seen the movie *Colors* and had heard about gangs all over Los Angeles, and here we were in Hollywood, meeting one for ourselves.

The guys in the black sweatshirts walked up to our table, paused for a moment, and then asked, "Hey, you guys in the Crucified?"

Ha!

The letters on the front of their sweatshirts read: "P.O.D."

They announced themselves as a band called Payable On Death, from the San Diego area, and said they were just starting out. Oh, of course. A band. I'm gonna go and change my shorts.

CHAPTER FIVE

We played the show that night, and even met the old man who owned the place, Bill Gazzarri, while he was walking around his bar and talking to the staff. He was a grouchy old buzzard, who got really pissed at us for doing our little preaching thing from the stage. At that point, half the band was still under twenty-one, and most of our crowd was, too. He was disappointed with the liquor sales, so he tried to make us give the club money for an imaginary chair he claimed was broken during our show. The security guys, who had been hanging out with us right before we played, said "Old Man Gazzarri" tried that all the time, so they helped us sneak out the back door. As we were leaving, Gazzarri yelled at us, saying, "I own this town—you'll never play in it again!"

The next few years, despite ol' Bill's warning, the Crucified continued to play Southern California. We played in Orange County, Ventura, and Los Angeles, but also further south to cities like San Diego, Temecula, and Oceanside— where we would have huge shows for a band our size, playing to as many as fifteen hundred kids. All of this happened with minimal radio play and an album that people could only get at shows. Back home, we managed to jump onto bills with bands like D.R.I., Pantera, and even third-wave ska pioneers (and San Joaquin Valley natives) Let's Go Bowling. We tried to reach out further, taking trips to Arizona— once to play with punk rock heroes G.B.H.—and the San Francisco Bay area, but for the most part, we were just trying to get the name of the band known at home and down south. Orange County was easier to play than Los Angeles, and soon enough, it became a kind of second home for us.

Shortly after our album came out, Mark Johnson, the

third bass player of the Crucified, had become a difficult
presence in the band, and we parted ways. Since Jim, Greg,
and I had been playing together for so long, it had been a
rough transition adding Mark to the band, and I felt bad
for him. I don't think he was ever comfortable with us, and
the situation finally reached the point where either he had
to leave, or the band would break up. I just think that for a
person like Mark, breaking into a circle that tight was too
much, and he went off to do his own thing.

Our friend, Roger Martin, the bass player of Vengeance,
called us up one day and told us about an ad he had seen in
a weekly L.A./O.C. entertainment magazine called *BAM*
that advertised upcoming shows and gave concert and
album reviews. It also had personal ads for people looking
for bands and others for those trying to fill spots. He called
us and said in his thick southern accent, "Hey man, you still
looking for somebody to play bass?" ("Hey" sounded like
"Hi" and bass sounded like "bice.") Jim told him yes, and
Roger read him the ad over the phone: "Guitarist looking
for band. Influences include: Slayer, Metallica, the Crucified,
blah, blah, blah. You should call this guy and see if he would
switch to bass for y'all." Jim called the number, and a guy
named Jeff Bellew answered the phone. He didn't believe
that it was Jim at first, but after Jim spoke to him for a few
minutes, Jeff had basically become our new bass player. He
tried out for the band, got the gig, and then drove up to
Fresno—four hours minimum—for practice every weekend. After the drive became too much, Jeff finally gave
in, poor guy, and left southern California to move up to
Fresno. ("Dude ... Fresno sucks.")

CHAPTER FIVE

CHRISTIAN PEOPLE AND THE WORLD OUTSIDE

The Christian Driver: Jeff Bellew was always a very sharp observer of bizarre tendencies common to the Christian community. Behind the wheel in Los Angeles at the peak of rush hour—probably going to El Dorado studios; after all, we spent a lot of time driving to El Dorado Studios—Bellew let out his signature sigh. "Hhhhhhh. Grr." The car in front of us, which had been tapping its brakes repeatedly for some distance, was slowing down beneath the flow of traffic. Riding the brake, brake lights on the whole time. Can't tell if they're stopping until you're suddenly two inches from their bumper. We could see the profile of the driver ahead of us, peering over her shoulder as if to change lanes. Signal comes on, signal goes off. Signal comes on, signal goes off. Speed up, slow down. After a couple more looks over her shoulder, signal still on, she stays in the lane in front of us.

"See that," he says, pointing to a "Jesus Fish" on the back of her car. "You know what that is, right?"

I wait.

"Bad-Driver's License."

Not that poor driving skills are exclusive to the Christian community—of course not—but it does make one think about impressions and the ever-present concern of "witness." I am a bad driver. I am impatient. I get distracted easily. These are all reasons why the back of my car displays … nothing at all.

The Christian Business Card: Or Company Van. Or Yellow Pages ad. Does the "Jesus Fish" bring business, or share the Gospel? Does it say, "I'm trustworthy," or "I'm in the Club?" Maybe it brings good luck. I'm just asking.

The Christian Diner:
Look, waiting tables is a lot more stressful than anyone

who has never done it might think. There is a lot more going on than just bringing out your meal. There are standards of service that the restaurant believes will keep people coming back; there is a ton of sidework (cleaning, stocking, maintaining) that goes on during even the busiest of times; there are people to tip out after the shift is over (tipping out: sharing the money left behind by the patron with bussers, food runners, and even hosts; often an amount designated by sales and not by the amount one actually makes from gratuity—if you suck at serving, why should everyone else have to pay for it?).

Everybody already knows that a table full of Christians will be a nightmare of people who: don't listen to you; don't acknowledge you; have a strong (however bizarre and displaced) sense of entitlement; don't tip. It is an accepted reality among food servers that Christians tip lousy.

Here's an idea: Tip well. Tip very well. You will be remembered. You will make a good impression. Your server might be the greediest, laziest person in the restaurant, but so what? How would you describe yourself in your work environment, or even ... before you were saved? If that's the level we have to start on, then so be it. When people were hungry, Jesus fed them. He met them where they were. What's a couple extra bucks to make a good impression on a person you just might have the opportunity to get to know someday? (Rule of thumb: 20 percent. Trust me, it gets spread around. Make somebody's day and see what happens.)

Oh yeah, for that person who invented the tract-disguised-as-a-twenty-dollar-bill, with the message inside (once the briefly ecstatic server opens it) that reads, "Expecting a tip? Well, here's something that will last you a lot longer than money: The Gospel ..." Don't let me catch you in a dark alley when no one's looking—I'm trying here, but I'm still human ...

SIX

WHERE IT FELL APART

The purpose of this book, as I stated from the beginning, is not to tell my life story. It's also not to defend the lives of decadent or licentious people. It's also not to make villains of those who don't know me, my life, or the lives of my peers and fellow artists. The purpose again, as I have already stated, is to show how many of us came to have our present mindsets. I'm hoping to share some perspective.

Part of understanding my mindset—which is just mine, but I think its one that is fairly close to that of many Christians in the entertainment industry—is to know how I am acquainted with sin and failure. If I can help you understand that then, ideally, this book will also help to explain why so many of us simply reject the weight of such an ambiguous title as "role model"—a term that imperfect people invented for other imperfect people. For those of you who think it's absurd of me to fear that tag, or if it just sounds vain ... well, all I can say is, I agree! Unfortunately, "Hey, you have to accept the fact that you're a role model because you're in a band, blah, blah, etc." is something I've heard for over half of my life now—and it's never seemed anything but absurd to me.

FROM THE GET GO

We are all trying to find our way along the paths God has chosen for us. We are all humans, subject to error.

I don't offer that as an excuse for anyone—including myself—but rather, to make a case for compassion. Trust me, it's needed in light of the realities faced by any group of human beings who are held to a higher standard by people who are looking for unerring role models. As American Christians, there is so much confusion when trying to weigh and balance our responsibilities as Christians and the responsibilities of those in the spotlight. For those in that spotlight, there is an assumed responsibility to do some greater good, as if, because of increased visibility, one is capable of more than the average person who is away from it. But now I'm getting off track ...

While this group of default leaders sometimes—inexplicably—includes entertainers, it has begun to exclude some of those people who are actually capable of filling this role: parents, teachers, and pastors. Their roles within the lives of the people who either look up to them, or depend on them, or are even taught by them, are completely different from the role of some singer in a band. The ability to play music is not a spiritual gift, at least not anywhere that I've read. Teaching and preaching are spiritual gifts, according to Scripture (Ephesians 4:11-12). And parenting ... is on a whole other level.

I believe that my parents, and most of the other spiritual leaders in my life, had the best of intentions. Unfortunately, being human, they couldn't possibly have done a perfect job raising me, teaching me, or leading me. Not only does that mean they didn't teach me everything I needed to know, which is understandable and something no reasonable person would expect, but unfortunately, it also means that some of the things they taught me were incorrect. Seeing as I still love my parents, pastors, and teachers—former and present—this is where the subject matter of this book becomes ... delicate.

Throughout my coming of age, when I was trying to develop as a Christian and as a young man, I was reminded at every turn not to run astray or fall prey to "the lust of the flesh and the boastful pride of life." Of course, this was sound, scriptural advice, but it didn't tell the whole story. I didn't learn until later that with just the slightest loss of focus, even while heeding warnings like those, a person could become full of pride and arrogance. With that slight loss of focus comes a change of motivation, and that's when things start to come apart. Obedience for the simple sake of obeying God can become replaced by the desire to be seen as "godly" by other Christians. I believe that this not only dishonors God, but also might be a kind of idolatry.

Be it for the praise of other Christians, or just to get them off your back, the desire to have people praise your progress in the faith can be just as vain as the need to be seen as a success by your peers, or society, or any of those other forms of "acceptable" ego-stroking. Since the very essence of God's grace is that He has given us unmerited mercy in return for our wickedness, ego should have nothing to do with our growth as Christians. I believe that taking pride in driving a better car or having a nicer house than your neighbor is no less a matter of pride as the desire to hear other Christians praise your so-called godliness. While it's good to encourage others by maturing in your faith, just as the spiritual maturity of those around us is encouraging, it's also easy to get off track. I'm talking about that need for a spiritual "Atta-boy!" or a better seat in church on Sunday, or the always dangerous acceptance into that inner circle of "church staff." (No, I don't think that the position of a

CHAPTER SIX

church staff member is evil, I just know that if Christianity is treated like a social club, it often has the same entanglements as one. From someone who spent half of his life growing up in churches, I can say it happens, and more often than you might think.) I've seen the pursuit of those types of positions breed all sorts of ugly behavior, turning guileless Christians into ambitious religious leaders.

I also feel qualified to hold this belief because I've lived this way—seeking the praises of other believers—and been guilty of this off-base thinking for much of my life. (I don't dare say that as if it were something I've completely conquered ...) It can breed self-righteousness and a false sense of security.

There is the potential to convince one's self of his own maturity in Christ, while in fact not maturing at all—maybe even losing some maturity—and leaving one's self susceptible to sin. It's false. It's puffery, and it's dangerous. It's dangerous because that sense of security will most likely disappear the moment an individual is no longer around people who care whether they are "godly" or not.

My direction was off from the start. At the beginning of my spiritual life, I basically adopted a religious heart. I was trying to be a better Christian, but by my own efforts. Soon enough, I was so lost in my own world, with no idea that was the case. I tried to live up to my own expectations, and eventually to the ones that were put on me by other people. We humans tend to pervert the purity around us in some way or another, and our relationship with God is no different. I tried to take back control of my own life in a way that many Christian people would say was positive. I was trying to be like God, but on my own. He was "continuing to perfect" the good work He had started in me, and instead of letting Him, I tried to take over.

The irony here is that I thought the little things I was doing to keep myself in line were making me stronger, but in fact, they were weakening a young and fragile Christian life.

I said what I thought I should say, rather than what I really felt. I would put on an act of naiveté, hoping my parents would be fooled, and not fear their son was going to end up the same kind of hell-raiser that they had been. I was still lying, but in a different form than I had before, and I don't think I realized what I was doing. I knew that I was hiding part of myself, but at the time, I thought that was just what I was supposed to do. I thought that was what people meant when they talked about setting their minds on the things above and putting their old ways behind them. What my parents thought of me meant so much that I did whatever I could to have them think the best of me, especially in light of all I had done while growing up.

If I talked about a movie or an experience, I would find a way to incorporate God or Jesus into it. I tried to maintain the appearance of someone who kept God at the forefront of his mind in everything, and I felt justified in my own weird little world of checks and balances. I thought that if I did these types of things, I would somehow become closer to God. Yes, I did turn away from some temptations, but not because I wasn't tempted or because I wanted to please and obey God, but because I didn't want to get into trouble. And it seemed to be working for a while ... but that type of religion never lasts for long.

It was a difficult time. Every day, I would go through the same series of failures. When you add into this my own maturing body and the confusion of puberty, it truly was a time of chaos. I believe my experience is probably common among many young Christians who are still growing up. We grow up dealing with our society, our bodies, and our faith, all at the same time. So, we try to please everyone—God, our families, and society—by attempting to live up to their expectations, real or imagined, and in the end, we feel like failures. Looking back now, this way of living was as sure a formula for alienation, inner turmoil, and the constant fear of letting yourself and others down as I can come up with.

I believe most of the confusion comes from trying to be a good person in the eyes of two different groups of people—those who are Christians and those who are not. But often what God wants from us, or what He calls righteousness, is the opposite of what our parents, teachers, and society would have in mind. Trying to please both groups of people can be like going in two different directions at once. It's so much simpler really: Be obedient to God. That is being a "good Christian." In trying to please everybody, I felt that I failed to please anyone, least of all God.

We are limited to what God does in us while in pursuit of maturity in our faith. All the effort we put into looking like good Christians is a waste of time, and in fact drives a wedge between God and us when it's done for false reasons ... I would definitely say it borders on dishonesty. We are impatient. We want to be declared "finished" immediately, and try to skip ahead to the end, because that sometimes works in the world we live in. For whatever reason, God only gives enough for today, for right where we are, and He simply will not let us look ahead or worry about the future. "Thy Word, is a lamp unto my feet, and a light unto my path" (Psalm 119:105). When that passage was written the only lamps people had were weak little things that lit the ground up around a person's feet. Just enough to keep them from stumbling. As I've heard countless pastors say, "The word flashlight does not appear in that sentence." There is a part of the path we weren't intended to see yet, and if we get caught up trying to see it by shining ahead with a flashlight we don't have, we lose track of where we're going. Soon, we end up so far off the path that we have to spend all of our time getting back on it. The straying is a process, but it doesn't take much to get it started.

The biggest fault on my part came in not holding to the standards God set as the highest ones, those to which all other standards must yield. All the guidelines we need for life are found in the Bible, and the standards we need to live up to are there as well. If we aren't content with those standards, we are already off of the course and headed for trouble. (It's a simple matter of trust and of faith. Do I believe that by obeying God and following where He leads, I will be content and safe?) Christians are still people. They— we—still have the tendency to want to achieve godliness in a way that will not just please God, but will also impress others ... and eventually that will create a conflict. Do we live up to the standards that man has set because we want to please God, or man?

THE HARD PART

As for me, I feel this downward spiral of the mind came about for two reasons: One, I was already a sinner, and two, because I was being taught by sinners.

There, I said it.

The job was incomplete. I knew that I was a sinner, that Jesus died for me, and that His resurrection was evidence of His deity. And I knew He forgave me for all of my sins. I knew these things, but I didn't know what to do with the information.

I guess I just wish someone would've told me how to take the information I had been given and then make it work. (Or that someone would have nailed my feet to the ground until I understood on my own.) I felt like a mechanic who'd been given all of the tools to fix a car—without being shown how to use any of them. If something was broken, I could have been holding the tool to fix the problem, and still not have known where to start. I didn't know how to sort through what mattered to me and what mattered to God. I was too busy most of the time trying to

CHAPTER SIX

not do the wrong thing. I knew how to not have premarital sex. How to not get drunk. I knew how to not embarrass my parents in front of other people at church. I just didn't know how to apply the teachings regarding spiritual maturity that I had heard in church to my life: How does one actively "set (one's) mind on the things of God" (Colossians 3:2)? How does one take hold of "the mind of Christ" (1 Corinthians 2:16)? I was too busy not cussing, not doing drugs, not hanging out with the wrong people, etc.

While still trying to understand what it meant to be a Christian and how to live a Christian life, I was told that I now had to go out into the world and lead others to Him. I was out in the field of battle without any real knowledge of how to fight, let alone teach someone else. I guess I would have liked a lot more room for error. For years I felt that with every move I made, the salvation of the world was at risk. I was taught that I "might be the only Jesus they will ever see." What is that? That's quite a responsibility for a new Christian, let alone a *kid* who was a new Christian. Is it an accurate one? I heard similar statements more often once the band became such a large part of my life. I went from being told to hand out tracts about our faith at school during lunch, to having people out in the crowd yelling, "Preach Jesus! Preach it, Brother!" If I didn't do this, in either situation, I was suspected of denying my faith and "just lettin' 'em march right into hell!" Did God entrust my salvation to the success or failure of some adolescent kid, or much less, a musician? Sorry, that doesn't work for me.

I tried to be a witness in this way, but the application of it made less and less sense as the days passed. I wasn't prepared once I had conversations with actual human beings who would ask me right in the middle of my big pitch, "So, did my mom go to hell when she died? She wasn't a Christian." I would tell the truth, but I needed lots of tries to state it in love, and with tact. I didn't know what I was doing!

So what am I saying? Am I accusing the Church as we know it of sending young people out into the world unprepared?

Yes.

And no.

None of us can see everything coming. As I said, I think we are all trying to find our way down the paths God has given us, and He only lets us see a little bit at a time. My parents were learning, too, and they were just as new to all of this as I was. My pastors were only leading in the ways that seemed the safest to them.

So what? What's the point? Good question. I think the point, in keeping focus on the intent of this book, is that people are imperfect. I address this here in hopes of gaining a little more grace from my fellow Christians. And for the same reasons I am looking for grace from strangers, I need to extend it to the people I interact with. (News flash: Your parents aren't perfect!) Anytime you are dealing with other people, it's completely unfair to assume they will live up to your expectations. You and I are simply not qualified to have expectations of others beyond the simple basics of the Bible, and even then, we have to keep in mind the reality that we are all still learning. We never know the whole story of a person's day—or life. I believe we need to be reminded of this because our natural tendency is to fall back on the default, finite wisdom we were born with, and that's when we start to put people on pedestals.

My parents didn't want to make the mistakes that they did in raising me, and I didn't want to make the mistakes I did while growing up. When you meet a musician on the road, how can you know what is going on in that person's life? How could anyone be so bold as to say things like, "He doesn't seem to be reflecting the joy of Jesus"?

Death in the family, rough day in the van, or maybe just a little discouraged by their own sin ... any of these reasons

CHAPTER SIX

should be good enough to remind us that we don't know everything. Life is too hard and all our paths are too difficult for us to hold a musician, an athlete, or even a long-lost friend to a standard we've created ourselves and justified in the name of Decent Christian Living.

Is it so hard to see why the term "role model" means nothing to me? I know me; I'm too acquainted with my sins, struggles, and weaknesses to take a tag like that seriously. Life is too short to try to live up to each person's standards of right and wrong. I can't be perfect in every eye, and maybe coming to that understanding now is one of God's little jokes—a way of paying me back for all of the times I expected perfection of others. But, now the good news: All of this is part of God's plan. All of it. God surely does work in mysterious ways, and all of His mystery still points to His glory and His sovereign power. Only God can take a person who feels the way I do, who's done the things I've done, and drop them into all of this apparent confusion—apparent—and then have it transform into something wonderful.

Unfortunately, the happy ending doesn't come until after the unhappy period right before it. It was hard to convince myself that life doesn't flow the way the movies I grew up on did. In a movie, despite all of my faults, I would end up redeeming myself just in time to be the hero. In real life, God is my redeemer, and regardless of what I do or don't do along the way, He is glorified—and He graciously forgives my sins and allows me into heaven, completely because of that grace.

Somewhere along the transition from the end of my high school years into my early adulthood and the independence of being on my own, I lost sight of who I was and what really mattered the most. I lost sight of the price of my own sins, and of the value of treating people the way they should be treated. I forgot that it really did matter whether or not we treat people like Jesus would. Can you imagine that?

I'm ashamed of the memories even now.

PAPER VIRGINITY

Meanwhile ...

I had remained a virgin all throughout my high school years, while all of my friends were discovering sex. I never felt that out of place. In fact, I felt normal; it seemed weird to me when a kid my age would talk about dating and sex. Being so sheltered, it was surprising for me to hear guys compare sexual escapades, and even stranger to hear girls talk just as frankly about sex—and stranger still to hear them get more explicit.

I was always around girls, especially on the swimming and water polo teams, which were co-ed, and they seemed comfortable around me. I was the Christian kid, and while the girls still had few reservations about making a move on a boy with a Bible in his backpack, they knew I wasn't going to be making any moves of my own, so I was "safe." (I later would be given a tongue-in-cheek nickname by some of my adult female friends: "The Gay Friend." Some of the girls mean it only jokingly, because they know I'm a Christian, but we all have a good laugh at the girls who think that because I don't cater to their attempts at pro-vocative behavior, I must be gay ...) I stayed a virgin, and it wasn't that hard. I just believed I would remain one until I was married, and that was it. I just didn't want to have sex, like I didn't want to steal, or I didn't want to push down little kids on the playground. I was also somewhat into the Straight Edge scene, at least the discipline of it, which, to most of us at the time, was really about not being con-trolled by drugs or alcohol ... or sex. People who couldn't keep their pants on for more than a first date were looked upon as weak-minded and pitiful. All of that helped, but to be honest, I just had a conviction in my heart to remain that way until marriage. It also helped that while I was still around my parents, going to church, and reading my Bible, I always knew I would be found out if I ever did lose my virginity. (Or do drugs, or ditch school, etc.) I also knew that the disappointment my parents would feel for me would far outweigh this mysterious activity called sex.

Those boundaries worked for a while. Then I discovered independence.

NOT WELL

Once out of high school, life didn't change much at first. College was just an extension of the same old life I was living while at high school, just with more girls and less boundaries. I held out for a while, but eventually the boundaries of accountability and parental supervision blurred, and the little protection from sins they provided wasn't enough.

Shortly after I turned eighteen, I moved out of my parents' house for about four months. I believe that the moment I left their close supervision, the downward spiral that was my relationship with God picked up speed, and it didn't slow down until about five years and a million sins later. I discovered that the same girls I used to hang with were sometimes looking to be more than friends ...

I moved back in with my parents after that summer, but couldn't stay under the watching eyes I had lived away from, and I moved right back out about a year or so later. I think the move home made the sins available to me out in the world that much more appealing. I had tasted that fruit of self-indulgence just enough to know it was there, and I went right back to it as soon as I was free of the controlling gaze ... but I always tried to keep up appearances. I couldn't stop going to church, because then they would know for sure!

But of course, as always, they did know. They had been watching every move I made ever since I was a kid. Now that I was an adult and most of the members of our family were Christians, they watched me even closer. Complicating things was the fact that my parents and I were in completely different places, and I knew it. I couldn't relate to them for all of the same reasons that most kids can't relate to their parents, but we had the whole spiritual aspect working against us, too. Living with them, my sin and my insecurities were getting tangled up all of the time, and I always ended up feeling like there was little I could do to please them. Sometimes there is a difference between sinning and just being a screwy kid, but it wasn't always clear, so I often felt caught in double jeopardy—I would forget to clean my room and pray for forgiveness from God for it. Something wasn't quite lining up.

There were other ways that Christianity compounded our generation gap problems, as well.

By the time they were eighteen, both of my parents were ... parents. They both had already been married and divorced by the time they were twenty-one or twenty-two. They also didn't become Christians until their early thirties. We had grown up in as many completely different ways from each other as we could have, and I had a difficult time trusting that. They didn't know what it was like to be a Christian and go through puberty and adolescence. And as a Christian, single, and living on your own? No way. Christian and not the coolest kid at school? Or how about ... being a Christian boy and only having relationships with Christian girls?

It started to really become a problem when they didn't fully support the band. From the beginning, I felt like I was doing something wrong in their eyes. My parents went to *one* show the Crucified played in all of our eight years—our first, and they left before it started. They had gone to the one K.G.B. played, but that was before I could even drive. They didn't trust the idea of me getting involved in music; I think they were afraid I would get caught up in some negative lifestyle or something ... I don't know. I resented it, though. I felt like I would never be able to earn their trust, no matter what I did. When I had completely fallen on my face, I feared the band would always be the trump card that was dropped, as if I was not only responsible for my sin, but the band was, too.

Punk rock certainly didn't help either. One day I had come downstairs from my room right when my dad came home from work, and we really had it out. I don't remember what started it, I think I had shaved my head, or I was wearing ugly clothing, or whatever. My dad, who had probably had a rough day on the job, came unglued. He said that by being into punk rock, I was in sin, to which I replied with a question, "How?" His response was that he couldn't stand it, that it made him angry, and therefore it was a stumbling block to him! I knew enough about our faith to know that was a bit of a reach. Then, while doing chores and listening to one of my smuggled tapes ... my dad caught me. I had disobeyed him, but he skipped right past the whole smuggling secular music issue and went straight to what I had suspected all along: taste. He said I couldn't listen to that sort of music because it wasn't Christian, but I could listen to the oldies station (that he listened to) because it was okay. I, of course, said that wasn't Christian either, and that all of those old songs were just about sex anyway. 'Round and 'round we went again.

Once again, we were all just learning. I know that now. I love my parents, but it was a strange way to grow up. I felt like a bad son and a bad Christian most of the time, and eventually I completely shut both of my parents off. I felt that even when my motivation was innocent, they were always looking for some hidden, sinful agenda on my part. I felt like we were building higher and higher walls between us. After a while, I built my wall to the ceiling. I still tried to keep them happy. I said the things I thought would make them realize I was a good Christian, while simultaneously expecting them to let me down. We were at that place where the more you do, the worse it makes everything, so you just do less, come around less, and try to stay out of each other's way.

When I started to fall away, I felt like the last thing I wanted to do was tell them anything. I was afraid that they would just shake their heads and say, "We always knew it." I refused to come to them for guidance because I had convinced myself that the most important thing for me to do was prove them wrong. Coming to them would be conceding.

A little humility would have gone a long way toward helping me with some of the troubles I was having, and it would have prevented a lot of the ones that came later. Allowing my parents to help would have been wise, but I wasn't wise. Looking back now, I see the kind of person I was, but I also see that the hard lessons I put myself through might have been necessary to teach me that humility and wisdom. I know my parents loved me, but we were both on unfamiliar territory, and I think we had reached the point where I just needed to go out into the world and learn on my own.

Of course, the best thing to have done when the situation started to come apart would have been to go straight to God, by way of His Word, and add in some honest fellowship along the way.

Problem was, I didn't do those things either.

I moved out of my parents' house for good at the age of twenty, and all of the boundaries that had kept me in line disappeared. I rented an apartment in Fresno with Greg and Jeff, who was now comfortably a member of the band. Jeff and I had become closer friends as the band grew and spent more and more time together. The three of us living in an apartment together seemed like a great idea. (It

CHAPTER SIX

wasn't. Here's another tip for you aspiring musicians: Don't live with your band. Before you know it, the band will be breaking up because someone didn't wash his or her dishes. If only our fans could have seen some of the exchanges between Jeff and me while we lived together ... they might wonder how we ever had any fun! With Jeff's wit and my temper? I seem to remember a hole being punched in a wall ... roughly the size of Jeff's head ...) A friend of ours named Steve moved in with us, just to sort of balance it out. Our place became the hub for loud parties and hanging out with all of our friends and girlfriends until the wee hours of the morning. In no time, my new home turned into the polar opposite of my parents' house, and you could say I let my inhibitions down. You also might say I dropped them entirely.

I don't blame the close supervision I was raised in for my fall—as if taking away boundaries rendered me powerless to resist yielding to the unseen and irresistible pull of my temptations—but I also don't want to lie in order to make the truth "nicer." I believe that I was not prepared for the real world. I also hadn't taken the responsibility for my own spiritual growth seriously when it would have been easiest, and so I fell on my face.

THE THREAD

Consistent with what had become my lukewarm life-style, I started going to a Bible study on Wednesday nights with some friends from Fresno City College and Fresno State University. Though I never grew too close to most of them—too much talk of Volvos and future domesticity for me—some of them did become friends. I just never felt at home in their group. I was the lone "punker" to them—yes, people really did use that CHiP's/Quincy/I Dig Pain/after school special term—but some of the guys were fun to hang around with, and the girls were attractive. (Being from a town as small Madera, there were hardly any girls, and even fewer Christian ones.) But the people who attended the group were from all over the country, and there was always an awkward, disconnected feeling in the atmosphere during their get-togethers.

Anyway, one weekend, some of us decided to check out a church close to Fresno State that was said to have a lot of people our age in the congregation, and that had apparently been reaching out directly to them. It was right around the corner from the apartment where I lived, so I thought I might give it a try. I went to the church, then the Bible study afterward. The study that weekend had been on sexual purity. The instructor said things like, "True love waits." (A catchphrase I always thought was weak. Why would you need to tell that to a Christian? Was that the best we could do to guard our children against peer pressure? Are the biblical commandments regarding fornication not enough ... yet this little catch phrase will be ...?) The teacher also had us tie small threads around our wrists and make a vow that we would not have sex until we were married—the thread was there to remind us of the promise we had made. College students. Thread around the wrist. I am writing this now and wondering if the guy shouldn't have just screamed at the top of his lungs, "You people are uncontrollable sexual deviants! I know how you are, because ... I'm one, too! Sorry about the whole thread thing, guys, we're just grasping at straws here! We have no idea how to keep all of you from hopping into the sack every time the lights go down! Carry on!" It was a clinic in desperation.

It was very strange, though—the moment I put that thing on my wrist, it was like a little voice went off in my head, saying, "You should probably just take that right back off. A short time from now, it will be ancient history." I couldn't describe it or explain where the certainty came from, I just knew it was true.

For the purposes of context, honesty, and making my point as clearly as possible, I will say this: Two weeks before my twenty-first birthday, I lost my virginity to a married woman, and was sexually active for the entire remaining years of the Crucified. I would sleep with a girl, ask God's forgiveness, then turn right back around and do it again. Once I allowed that part of my life to supersede my convictions, I did little to stop it. I felt lonelier during this time than I ever had, and I'm sharing this because I know there are people who have felt (or are feeling) the same way. I hope this helps you to know that you aren't alone. Simple as that. I'm also sharing this so that you can see how far back the cynicism that I will explain later goes.

When I lost my virginity, I was so depressed and so convicted that I wanted to confess my sins to anyone and everyone—I think I hoped I would find some peace. I didn't confess much though, because I knew if I did, anyone I would trust to confess to would be sure to halt everything that was going on with the band. Deep down, I knew I had no business being in the Crucified, but I justified it by telling myself that I would turn things around. And so, I kept going to church, praying to God, reading my Bible, etc.

I know there will be those people who read this who will attempt to make an issue of the "guilt" that must seem to cover my life like a blanket ... what can I say to that? I'm not Catholic, and I have no understanding of the term Catholic Guilt, but I do know what I believe: God's Word is true and righteous, and especially as a Christian who has tasted both God's grace and the benefits of following His Word, I feel guilty when I disobey that Word because ... I am guilty. Guilty of consciously disobeying Him.

It's really not complicated. It's not like some dark maze of words and rules used by "THEM" to oppress me. I believe the Bible is the Word of God, and I believe logic dictates that if part of it is considered true, all of it has to be considered true in order for it to be a consistent source of truth. If not, how do you know what you can really trust? What parts do you believe? I think when you are dealing with the supernatural, you need to believe completely, or why believe at all?

I wanted to tell somebody what was going on with me because I wanted to find some sort of release for that guilt ... and that might be the saddest part of all. I could have just gone to God; I knew He would have comforted me. The problem was, with God's comfort would come His correction. If I owned up to where I was spiritually, I would have to change, and whenever that thought came around, I buried it however I could.

I continued to preach at every show. Can you believe that? I preached out of habit, not out of conviction or passion or calling. Just because. And, not ever thinking that God might have a small problem with a person who was speaking out in His name as a child of His, and living a life of sin. I don't know that I ever wanted to preach, or cared enough for the souls of the lost to be good at it. I just kept up appearances and continued to receive the praises of those who approved of the part of my life I allowed them to see. It never occurred to me that I might be a joke, a hypocrite. I loved to create music and to play it live so much that I never wanted to admit to myself that I had no business being in anything called a ministry—something we in the Crucified had always claimed to be.

The details of my sexual activity are obviously private and not the easiest topics to talk about ... but who would need to know the details anyway? What I will say is that once the seeds had been given time to grow, it was too late. I allowed a little sin to exist—the little bit I could get away with without my parents finding out—and then once I was living away from them, those sins gave way to new ones. One sin goes well with another. And another, and another

... It took time, I suppose we tend to stray in increments, but eventually, the seeds I had sown brought forth a harvest. A step further than I had ever gone one night, a step further the next, and before I knew it, I wasn't just off of the path, I was lost.

But all the while I was a Christian, and as I drove that wedge in between my Savior and me, the separation from Him grew more painful. I became more and more afraid as I became less and less sure of my relationship with Him. What Christian wouldn't? (That's also what happens when you stray, right?)

How do we forget that fellowship with Him is where true contentment lies? Well, I forgot. It would be years until I would remember again. Had I been in close enough fellowship with someone whom I could talk to at this point in my life, maybe things would have been different, but I wasn't. I think there were some doors that I needed to go through alone, with only God at my side. I think that those are the times when God's strength on our behalf is shown—even if the way He does it is to break us. I also think that those who were closest to me could see that only God could help me at that point, and so maybe they stepped back, prayed, and waited for God to be God.

To the naked eye, things seemed to pick up for the Crucified. We got a call from Greg Sostrum again. This time he wasn't calling for himself, but to tell us he knew a guy who was building a record label and studio, and that he was interested in us. His name was Freddie Piro, and he was the owner of Ocean Entertainment. Sostrum set up a meeting for us at a show we were going to be playing in Hollywood, and Freddie came out and introduced himself. We made a little conversation, then went into the club to play the show. Apparently Freddie liked what he saw. We signed with his label shortly after and recorded our second full length album, *Pillars of Humanity*.

Now, by this time, around the end of 1991, a lot of bands had sprung up around southern California, and a sometimes healthy, sometimes ugly competition developed. One night, we were to be "co-headlining" with a Christian speed metal band in Reseda, at a place called the Country Club. A band called Scaterd Few (sic) was going to open the show. When we got into the club, the speed metal band, we'll call them ... Black Spandex, informed us that we would be opening for them, by way of a rather lopsided promotional poster, and worse—the marquee. There was a bit of tension and pettiness, probably coming from both camps. ("Could you please go to your own dressing rooms ... this one is ours, it's for the headliners," etc.) We were pissed, mostly because we had just finished our album and wanted to make a good impression on Freddie Piro, who showed up at the gig with his wife and daughter. It wasn't a real big deal; we figured we would rather just play instead of making an issue of it—and hey, if Black Spandex had "the big draw," then we would at least be guaranteed to have both their crowd and ours.

Scaterd Few, a band that had recently reemerged from back before the Crucified, played the first slot, which was not an easy thing to do when half of the crowd is full of testosterone pumping knuckleheads, who don't understand why the singer is wearing a lace skirt and burning incense on the stage. (A guy named Ramald Domkus—now known by his real name, Alan Aguirre—and his brother Omar fronted them. Scaterd Few was a great band that did their fair share of ruffling the feathers of uptight Christian people, what with their make-up, dresses, dreadlocks, and such. They were extremely tight, thanks to a drummer who Jim used to love to watch named ... Sam West, and to Omar's amazing skills on the fretless bass.) As usual though, their music—a mixture of Bowie, Jane's Addiction, and maybe a touch of i against i-era Bad Brains—went over well. When we got onto the stage, the crowd was wound-up and rowdy.

The show went sort of out of control when the music started. A pit developed in the middle of the crowd immediately, and there were kids stage diving and crowd surfing all over the place. About halfway through the show, out of the corner of my eye, I caught sight of a young guy who had jumped onto the stage just long enough to launch himself even higher into the air, and then back out onto the crowd. A cool looking thing to see, I guess, until he landed on his face and didn't get up. Everybody in the pit stopped moving and told us to stop playing, something was wrong. Right then Bob Beeman, the pastor from the metal church, who had been at the show because Black Spandex was one of his Sanctuary-affiliated bands, jumped on the stage. He had been a little overwhelmed as things were, what with the atmosphere of the show and the tension between so many different people from such totally different scenes, all together in one building. He took the mic and, with the best intentions, told the crowd not to do what they had been doing ... no more dancing, no more stage diving, and all of that ... things were getting too dangerous, etc. This really didn't go over well with the crowd, who were used to people getting knocked around at shows, and the atmosphere in the club turned from fun to uncomfortable. By the time we got back on track, the kids at the show weren't sure what they could and couldn't do, and we just had to power through the set anyway. By the end, everyone was back at it. We finished and got off of the stage.

(Later as I walked through the crowd, I found the poor "kid" who had hurt himself: He was sitting in the lap of a pretty girl, who was inspecting his face for any scratches or blemishes. When he saw me, he jumped out of her lap and onto me, then nearly hugged me into a coma. He told me his name, Kelé, and he let me know that he was just fine. We became instant friends, and have remained so, even though these days we rarely see each other ...)

Freddie was happy, and our fans got a mostly fun show with lots to talk about. By the second or third song of Black Spandex's set, half of the crowd was gone.

All of this happened exactly one year and one day to the day that Bill Gazzarri, who told us we would never play "his town" again, passed away. A month after our show, Slayer played at the Country Club, and word was that someone in the band urinated on a wall during their set. The Country Club didn't book another heavy band again.

Much later into our mini-reign in southern California, we booked a weekend of shows with Gary Nixon, our newest, and last, manager. His idea: Make some waves by selling out three nights in a row, and maybe we can get some attention.

The first night was a Friday, and we played in Tustin to a sold-out crowd, but the stage was outdoors, and nobody really felt that great about the show itself. The next night we played in Anaheim, and once again, the show was full, but nothing about it was too memorable, although I do think that was our first exposure to a band called Focused, with a bass player named Dirk Lemmenes.

The last night of this three-day run was the show that I think solidified our status as a headlining band in the L.A./O.C. area. We were in southern Orange County in a town called Laguna Beach, playing at a place called "Club Post Nuclear."

We played with Scaterd Few and some local opening bands. As Scaterd Few were playing their set, I snuck outside to see the crowd, which, according to the rumor floating around the club, was bigger than the one inside the sold-out five-hundred-seater. (There were definitely five hundred people, standing anywhere they could, probably pushing all sorts of legal limitations. The walls and the floor alone, covered in condensation from the heat coming off of all of the people sweating profusely, had to be some kind of health hazard.) I came out just in time to see a young man jump from the roof of one of the neighboring buildings into the crowd that waited outside. I saw another kid jump from a telephone pole into the waiting crowd below, only not with the same success, as it appeared that only the few guys who came with him bothered trying to catch him. Despite a few scuffles with people who were upset at not getting inside, the crowd seemed content finding their own way to have a good time. They weren't going to get in, the show was sold out, and so they all just hung around outside the club. And there really were more people outside than there were in.

We got the attention we needed … sort of.

WINNING BATTLES, LOSING WARS

During the last four years of the Crucified, I found myself completely off track, and I didn't recover until all of the damage I could do had already been done.

The Crucified played, and grew, steadily up until 1992, and we could sense something "big" just out of our reach. Then the impact of our sins started to show. I think in my case, that elusive "something" kept me just occupied enough to not notice that God was bringing everything to a close. We accomplished many of the goals we set for ourselves, but apart from what God may have done in spite of us, all of those accomplishments and all of that progress amounted to nothing … nothing.

Another awkward moment passes
catering to questions asked by you
I do believe I've told you what you want to hear
It's so easy to recite
the lines and lies I've memorized
from this pedestal pushed through the sky
I'm laughing at your face
I hate who I am
and all that I've become
Many sleepless nights have found me
wandering comfortless streets
in search of peace—any release
from who I have become
and I'm sure you don't want to know
I hate the role, I'm old and cold
an ugly sore, a gaping hole
God have mercy on my soul
… are you disenchanted by the idol's humanness?
do you still think we connect?

"DEVIL"
Stavesacre, *Friction*

CHAPTER SIX

SEVEN

So, How are you doing?

As a child, I used to read a lot of comic books, something I think may have permanently affected me throughout life ... seriously. I spent much of my life halfway believing that one day I would rid the world of evil, perform amazing acts of physical superiority, and have the Adonis-like body structure of a Marvel super hero. My favorite comic book character of all time would have to be Spiderman. (I had a very brief moment when I considered not putting this in here, what with the movie and all. I guess I figured that for anyone as dedicated as I was, omitting this for the sake of not sounding trendy would just be a selling out. So there.) One of Spidey's many special powers was the always-valu-able "Spidey-Sense." There was Spiderman, on some impos-sibly high skyscraper wall, minding his own business and protecting the world from crime, and then all of a sudden, he would have a little buzzing halo around his head. "Uh-oh, Spidey Senses tingling! Danger is near!" This particular special power, aside from super-strength and practically being able to fly, is one I have wished I possessed countless times.

CHAPTER SEVEN

I'm on tour with Stavesacre, standing outside a show, when a young man approaches me with a look I can now spot about thirteen miles away, a look that says the person wants me to know how thoughtful and intense they are. A look that says to me: *RUN! Spidey Senses Tingling.*

"Hi Mark. How are you?"

Polite small talk is exchanged. (Small talk. Ugh. I'll try not to bore you with my standard answers to questions I find ugly and redundant in their unimaginative banality. Yes, I said banality.)

". "

"So hey, I wanted to talk to you about something."

" ... ?"

"Well, you mentioned to me at a show once that you had been seeing a girl now for some time, and—"

Okay, sorry, but I have to step in here and say to all aspiring musicians who happen to be reading this: No matter how tempting it might be, no matter how normal and approachable you want to be (or to appear to be ...) NEVER, EVER present personal information about yourself to fans as if you were talking to a trusted friend. You must at least control the way it's being presented, and to the best of your ability, the way it will come back. Your tact, common sense, and common courtesy are not shared by all. Some, many, MOST of these people will live all over you in ways that you never thought a decent person would ... trust me. You Do Not Know These People. They are not old friends. Okay, back to the story ...

"—Well, I just thought I would ask, I suppose to sort of keep you accountable, how are you two doing?"

"!?!?" (!$@#★!?)

"Well ... I just thought, you know, I would ask ... that's all. You know, how are you two doing with the premarital sex stuff?"

" ... ?" (!)

"What do you mean, how do I see it as my place to ask this? I mean, we are supposed to hold each other account-able, right? What, do you think you're above that? I was just ..."

The conversation ended with me walking away and scratching my head, not as much at the actual question, which just blew right past me, but more so at the presump-tuousness being displayed.

TOP FIVE ALL-TIME TOURING FILMS

(Very good for developing codes, which come in very handy for saying what you really need to say, when you really need to say it.)

5. **Planes, Trains, and Automobiles.** Steve Mar-tin and John Candy. Jeff Bellew used to love to say, "You can't get there from here." We've never really been lost, but we've sure had a hard time getting where we needed to go.

4. **The Royal Tenenbaums**. Dark humor is a bit of a theme for working musicians ... it happens. Wes Anderson is good for you.

Margot: "Do you send my mother your clip-pings? And your grades from college?"

Eli: "Please stop belittling me."

Eli: "You never gave me the time of day until I started getting good reviews."

CHAPTER SEVEN

Margot: "Your reviews aren't that good."
Eli: "But the sales are."

3. Tie: **Grosse Pointe Blank** and **High Fidelity**. John Cusack. Both are perfect. And somehow
related, beyond Cusack.

"So ... you wanna go somewhere else?"
"Yes." —*Grosse Pointe Blank*
"I don't have that record, I'll buy it from you for
forty."
"Bro, sold."
"Now why would you sell it to me and not to
him?"
"Because you're not a geek, Louis."
"Man, you guys are snobs." —*High Fidelity*

2. **Groundhog Day**. Bill Murray. If you don't
know, you never will.

"So, did you go pro with that whole belly-button
thing?"
"No, you will never guess what I do. I sell life
insurance!"
"What ... a shock."

1. **Quick Change**. Again, Bill Murray. A Clas-
sic. Under-appreciated genius. Every sarcastic line
from Bill Murray's character, Grimm, is appropriate
at some point in the touring process. You'll know
you've arrived when you appreciate the characters
with small parts. Still not on DVD, but it will be. It
better be. Or someone will pay, and dearly.

"Grimm, you have a gun. Shoot them."

"I would, but they're fur-bearing. I'd need some
sort of permit, wouldn't I?"

EIGHT

Where it died

By the time my actions caught up with me, I had spun
so far out of control that the only way I was going to come
down from the clouds was for God to shoot me out of the
sky. I knew He would not allow me to continue on, but instead of accepting that wisdom, I tried to run away from it.

SUPERSTITION IN THE CAMP

Right before one of the two or three "tours" the Crucified ever went on, we got together at Jim's house to pray
with Bruce Mumper, the pastor of Calvary Chapel of
Fresno. At that point, all of the band was attending church
there. We wanted to be spiritually focused and prepared for
the trip, and since prayer is the method Christians use to
speak to God—and hopefully to prepare to hear back from
Him, either through the Bible or through life itself—we
thought meeting with our pastor was the best idea.

We all knelt together in Jim's living room and prayed
our prayers out loud. We asked for strength to withstand
temptation and to be obedient, and for wisdom to make

good decisions. I don't remember what else we asked for ... or really why we were asking for those things. The temptations we faced on the road were the same ones we faced any other day, while at home or while working our jobs. There were no groupies, there were no drugs offered—or whatever other temptations are supposedly draped around the neck of the rock 'n' roll world—there were only the every day temptations of lust, greed, pride, etc. Not that praying for strength to overcome these everyday temptations is bad—it's absolutely necessary—but we were setting aside a specific time to address those concerns because it seemed like we should. Obedience is something I struggle with even still today, and have ever since I surrendered my will to Jesus. So, why the special attention?

We could have been praying about these concerns every day, and probably had been in one way or another, but addressing them in a group, and with someone who could act as a witness to it all, would satisfy our latent superstitions. (And oh yes ... in our own way, a lot of Christians are often just as superstitious and afraid of the "jinx" as anyone else.) A tour for us then, and really any show we played or music we recorded, had begun to seem like the proverbial "last key" we needed in order to open the door of success ... and we didn't want to screw it up. I started to see the Promised Land around every corner, and I think everyone in the band had been feeling the same way. Even something as simple as having our pastor over for a special prayer session seemed like a point we could look back on later as some crucial part of the puzzle that would eventually make up our success.

I will offer this in our defense: Having our pastor over did give us a little needed comfort. Going on the road was such a huge event in those days. There was so much we didn't know about the world outside of ours, and going out there with no security blanket was frightening. We had no idea what we were going to encounter, who we were going to meet, or whether or not anyone would even notice us out there in the big wide world.

When we finished praying, we all sat up and opened our eyes. As I remember, Bruce remained bowed and with his face to the ground. We all just kind of looked around ... I'm sure I even sort of half-bowed again, as if to avoid being caught breaking form or etiquette. After a while, Bruce stopped praying and sat up. With tears in his eyes and a trembling voice he asked us:

"What about love? What about the souls of these people you guys are supposed to be concerned for? What about them?"

I don't remember what we said. I do remember feeling defensive and misunderstood, but I don't remember doing much about it. For people so committed to being the perfect witness, to have such a huge question go by relatively un-addressed and unnoticed was indicative of where we truly were spiritually. I believe that by that time, God had the blinders on my eyes, and my course was set. I was going to go to the end of this the hard way, and moments like this one were probably there more for the sake of perspective.

After the season of rebellion had passed, we all would have been able to look back on the time God tried to wake us up from our spiritual sleep. I'm sure we probably said something that made us all feel better ... but the train moved on.

THE SOLO PROJECT

As if it wasn't enough to be totally involved in one band and completely lost in my faith, I decided to do more ...

A little more than a year after the Crucified put out *Pillars of Humanity*, I had the brilliant idea to do my own album. I had been listening to a lot of hip-hop and had fallen in love with the music.

Maybe too much.

Actually ... definitely too much.

I had grown weary of all of the hardcore, all of the speed metal, all of the same old same old. I still liked playing the shows, probably always would, but I just wanted to do something else. I had been listening to rap music, and a lot of old soul. I loved the raw energy and feeling of Al Green and Sly and The Family Stone. (Obviously inspired by my earlier love for Fishbone, who made no effort to conceal the influence Sly had on their music.) For me, all of the personality in their voices was the hook, something hard-core bands weren't exactly known for. I had also developed an appreciation for the sounds of some of the newer hip-hop groups coming up back then, especially Public Enemy and the second era of the Beastie Boys.

I wanted to make an album that would show off all of the music I loved. Sounds innocent enough, right? Well ... I guess there was some purity to my love for the music, but mostly I was looking for one more ego stroke. I was going through a major identity crisis, and at the same time I was trying to do anything I could to keep from getting a job.

The problem with going through an identity crisis when you are already an entertainer is that when you go through it, it's not in the comfortable anonymity of your bedroom, where no one else but your immediate family will witness it. Oh no ... I had mine on albums and posters that were distributed all over the country.

The project "Native Son and the Foundation" was a ridiculous mistake. It was bad rap music, if even that, made by a guy who knew nothing about the art form, except that he loved it. The thing is, loving something doesn't make you good at it. Loving movies doesn't mean a director will make good movies; the filmmaker has to be skilled at the art form. I love football, but I've got no business being out on the field with the Oakland Raiders. Hip-hop is hard. It takes style, not style as in class, but style as in style. Technique. A friend of mine named Peace was one of the few people who were honest with me during those deluded years. Once, while sampling my new tracks for the album, he told me I had no style ... and that was my style. It was a nice way of asking me just what in the world I thought I was doing.

I wanted to do something unexpected. When the fans of the Crucified found out I was doing a "rap" album, they immediately assumed I would do something like Rage Against The Machine. Looking back, I wish they had been right. It would have been easier to understand, and forgive. When the Native Son album came out, what the fans got was a confused, floundering piece of crap that was all over the place, and yet nowhere—all at once.

Yeah, do you feel that? I think they call it learning the hard way.

I played about five shows, I won't even get into those catastrophes, but let's just say that if it weren't for people like Pigeon John (then of the L.A.-based Brainwash Projects, then of LA Symphony, now a solo artist) and a group called A.W.O.L. Society (a couple of guys named Keith and Deric who were way ahead of their time) carrying the show, I would have been standing on the stage with no idea what to do. They gave the shows personality, and to be honest— some dignity. I was also lucky to have Edie Goodwin singing backups. Edie still sings in the punk rock band Headnoise and remains a friend. (And by the way, she still has an awesome voice.) My friend XL from the hardcore/hip-hop group Death Before Dishonor played drums, and kept the shows from being a complete horror. (DBD actually toured with the Crucified once. Hilarious. XL was a big man, who at one point in the early '90s sported a twelve-inch afro with a red, black, and green target painted on it.)

What was I doing, playing a live hip-hop show? I knew that I wanted a big group onstage, like I had seen in all of the old Sly, Parliament Funkadelic, and Tower of Power footage. I had seen Public Enemy's live show, but I knew I wanted a live band and a less serious image on stage. I wanted the shows to be parties onstage, and some were ... eventually. But really, what business does a singer—who can't even play an instrument in the first place, let alone orchestrate an entire show—know about playing that music live?

I was terrified, and every time I played live with Native Son, I told myself I would never do it again. I had no idea what to do. I needed volume and distortion to feel at home on a stage, and soon Native Son was history ... just not soon enough.

My friend Paul, the guy who owned Ragin' Records, was a huge hip-hop fan, among many of his other favorite styles of music. He once paid me this "compliment": "Well ... I think you do hip-hop better than Ice-T does rock 'n' roll." Think about that for a minute. Sounds like a compliment, but really ...

To this day, people still come up to me at shows, with Native Son CDs in hand, thinking they are quite witty and clever. I will take this opportunity to say: That joke sucks. It's really not funny, or witty, or original. Yes, I made a rap record. Yes, I wish I hadn't. But, y'know ... so what. Let's see you do it. Show me your latest album and then show me your copy of Native Son ... and I'll thank you for buying it. (Even if you only paid ninety-nine cents ... "A Bargain At Twice The Price!")

While there was blind arrogance all over that project, there was a little something in it, just a little, that was redeeming about the experience: I was forever free from the closed off room of zero creativity that, to me, was hardcore.

And, I actually did something. I did something that I was afraid to do. Later on, especially in the early stages of Stavesacre, that came in handy.

I also learned about my own arrogance and skewed view of the way things really were. Now I just see Native Son as "negative resistance training." When you lift a barbell to work out your biceps, the strain of lifting the weight up is the positive resistance, the part of the exercise that is obvious. The not so obvious part, is the strain of slowly letting the weight fall back into place. Negative resistance. That's how I see the Native Son fiasco: It taught me a lot about the parts of myself that needed changing—on the way down.

HEY! WANNA SEE A VOLCANO BLOW UP IN MY FACE?

The Crucified played a show down in Irvine, California, at a huge indoor stadium called the Bren Events Center. It was a weekend festival at UC Irvine, with tons of bands from all over the country coming to play. There had been a shift in the climate of southern California Christian music, with some of the older bands that we had grown up listening to passing on, and a lot of the younger bands coming up. We were playing bigger and bigger shows, and more and more kids were showing up. The old bands we listened to in more desperate times were just kind of ... fading.

The promoter of this "festival," whose name I don't remember, was freaking out because the attendance was horrible (eight hundred or so, in a place that holds more than five thousand ...) and he was in deep for the building. He was also committed to a lot of cash for the bands, and everyone knew that they probably weren't going to get paid, but none of us really cared. The guy promoted it well, the show just couldn't do much. The music scene, even in southern California, still wasn't developed enough at that point to justify huge venues and lavish shows. Bands like ours weren't too upset though, because we were still selling tons of merchandise. And while the show was small for the venue, it was still a great turnout for bands our size.

The day the Crucified played, all of the younger hardcore and punk bands sort of took over. Almost all of the fans who showed up came for those kinds of bands, and even for some of the hip-hop groups that were springing up. On the punk rock and "alternative" side of things, there were bands like ourselves, the Prayer Chain, truly "hardcore" Focused, Mortal, Scaterd Few, etc., and on the hip-hop side, there were groups like Freedom of Soul, SFC, and a few others. The Altar Boys and Undercover had been the biggest bands around in the earlier days, but their music had always been a little too soft for our crowds, and they were all moving on to other things. I guess we all felt like it was our turn.

All sorts of changes were happening. As if to underscore those changes, the promoter of the show came up to us halfway through the second day, when we were supposed to play at about five in the afternoon, and asked us if we wouldn't mind playing last.

Headlining. Whoa.

Most of the kids there were ours, and the Altar Boys— who were supposed to headline much later that night—had to leave early. I still remember sitting at our table in the dressing room, the terrified promoter hunched over the back of a chair, which he sat on backward, attempting to appear "relaxed."

He asked, "Okay, guys ... So and So of Such and Such has to leave early because he has this thing at this place up in L.A., and this ... is my vision: (hands held out, palms down) The show is here (hands patting down the air), right? Band A will play here, band B will play, then the Altar Boys are here (the whole time he's slowly putting his hands into a peak, like a little volcano), dig? Next, we'll have band Q play (hands come together in the shape of a volcano, fingertips touching), band Z (tips of fingers are together, but trembling), then band X. (Fingers stop trembling), and then ... closing the show ... the Crucified! (fingers explode upward ... volcano style.) Whadda ya think?"

We talked it over and decided that if the guy was going to humiliate himself doing the whole volcano-with-the-hands-thing, the least we could do was play along. Our fans and friends weren't too stoked on our decision, but most of them stuck around for our big "headlining" show.

It was flattering, kind of, so we agreed.

This would be my big show, see?

I needed it ... because I had this little problem.

Yeah, I had this little problem, and I needed to drum up some sympathy before the jig was up: My girlfriend at the time thought she might be pregnant.

By this time, I was one of the most selfish people on earth, and I had planned and plotted my spin for the situation. I had planned to go up onstage at our next big show and say I had been "going through some really scary things ... things that reminded me that I was a sinner, etc." What a jerk.

The unspoken policy within the band since its very beginning, when a former member had gotten his girlfriend pregnant, was that out of respect for the "witness of the band," anyone in similar circumstances was out. No real debate, just out. I don't know if that was a righteous or self-righteous way of handling sin, but it was just what had been decided. Instead of addressing the situation honestly and humbly, I had already begun to backpedal, trying to save my own skin and keep my pride intact.

While I was trying to manipulate the situation to my benefit, I continued to pray and beg God for mercy, grace, and "the woman time."

How stupid can one guy be? How selfish? I was actually seeking comfort rather than repentance, and in the process was oblivious to my disgusting behavior. Right around then (coincidentally? Are you kidding? I don't believe in coincidence, even when that belief would favor me) I had been reading in the Bible about God showing Moses the Promised Land he would never enter because he had misrepresented Him (and might have even tried to take some of God's glory for himself) at the waters of Meribah (Numbers 20 and Deuteronomy 34). I had been wondering whether or not God was doing the same thing to me. I was misrepresenting Him, and I still insisted on using God and the Gospel for my own ambitions, even to the point where I forgot that God doesn't share His glory. I was on dangerous and unfamiliar ground, and I could feel my sin catching up to me.

There we were, about to headline a huge place (forget the fact that the show was a disaster ...) and I was looking out over the stadium and wondering what it would be like if the band continued at its present course. I wondered if God was showing me what I could have accomplished, but had ruined for myself. (Forget my girlfriend, forget my potential child. Forget the damage that I would have done with my family, my friends, and the fans of the band. No, this was all about Mark, and whether or not I was going to get what I wanted.) I never saw my error, other than that it had presented me with a major inconvenience, and I never thought that maybe, just maybe, God wanted to help me—not just punish me for doing wrong, but maybe even help me become a man who would want to do right.

When it came time for us to play, I had it all planned out. I would say something sort of cryptic about my own life and my own sins, planting the seeds for a future harvest of forgiveness from the Christian community at large. In my out of control imagination, all the fans would remember what I said at the show, and once they found out what had happened, all would be forgiven. The wheels of compassion would have already begun rolling—that's why they call it "spin"—and by the time my sin was found out and shouted from the rooftops, I could just jump to the head of my own sad parade, and ride out on the comfortable cushions of sympathetic fans. Maybe I would make the subject matter for the next album all about my new found respect for sin or self-control or who knows what ... once again, just writing the truth about myself makes me nauseous.

When I think about how patient and gentle God is, I am amazed. When I read back over this part of my life, remembering the way I used to think, I'm still surprised that a lightning bolt didn't just shoot down from the sky and consume me. Sometimes I wonder if He just lets us dig our own holes—but I guess there's a bit more to it.

As the Bren Center show continued on, the atmosphere grew more and more crazy.

The stage was set up on the bottom of the arena, and the crowd took up most of the rest of the arena floor and a few of the surrounding bleachers. There was a huge barrier between the stage and the crowd, which was a real atmosphere killer—it took the crowd right out of the show. In a full-capacity setting, it would have been totally appropriate, but in this situation, with what felt like a small turnout, it was just silly. Who was going to get crushed? Who was going to rush the stage? Nobody. But in this case, everyone was so pissed off about the way the show was set up that all the punks and the hardcore kids—who by nature tend toward a predisposition that gives petty rules and restrictions the ol' one-fingered salute—were doing anything and everything they could to make the organizers sorry for making the show lame.

Not only was there the huge barrier between the crowd and the stage, but there was also a floor covering made up of these huge puzzle-piece type rubber mats that interlocked—to keep the Bren Center's hardwood floor from getting marked up—and there were rows of chairs all the way up to the barrier. I have to say that I was slightly more than amused to see those rubber mats spinning across the crowd like giant Frisbees. Some of the fans started pulling the seats up off of the floor—in rows of five or six blue, interlocked, plastic chairs—and passing them up and back over the crowd, hand over hand, like an assembly line. (I know for a fact that I saw Tim Mann, the singer of Focused, sort of orchestrating this mild protest ... and laughing like a little kid.) The truth was: Everyone was sick and tired of standing around, and they were a little stir-crazy. There was a kind of collective relaxing after a whole day of awkwardness, and everyone just wanted to let off some steam. We watched and laughed along with them. And then of course, after fifteen bands had played all day long and the show's millions of hitches, we were delayed coming onto the stage ... not good. The fans were nearly out of control, impatient, and chanting our name. You could see trouble coming if the show didn't get going.

Something that was very common in those days was to have about fifty people onstage while you played your set. I don't know, maybe it felt like a privilege for some people, but for myself and for a lot of our friends, the whole mini-phenomenon was fun. We wanted to be onstage to see our other friends playing their sets, while we could also watch the kids in the crowd go crazy. That day, everyone still left in the building was a friend of either someone in the band, or a friend of a friend, etc. I remember walking past Peace while he and his deejay, Cartoon, sat to the side and just sort of people-watched. I think XL was there, too, along with some of his friends ... everyone was there, just goofing off and having fun. It was a genuinely good time, despite the delays and the corny posturing that had gone on all day, and I missed it. I was all about saving my backside. I was focused, grim, and clueless.

Peace was this sort of mischievous type of guy, and I caught a sideways glance of him as I walked up the stairs to the stage. I still had the weight of the world on my shoulders and was still trying to figure out how I was going to make my move. Peace looked up at me and said, "Hey. Smile, dummy." No. No smiling from the Kid. All business.

We played the first five or six songs, the crowd went crazy, and it was probably the best show I ever played and missed completely. I wasn't paying attention, because I felt my opportunity was slipping past me. I couldn't just force my big speech into a break between songs ... I wanted it to come off natural and appropriate, and I needed everyone's full attention. We had a song called "Path to Sorrow" that had a solemn tone, being about the loneliness and alienation of a life without God. (Something I didn't really know or understand how to write about, but hey, that never stopped me before. It captured what most Christian kids thought a life without God surely must be like, and therefore was called, "A great song, lyrically." Ugh.) I thought it might be just the right place to give my speech. The song was coming up, maybe two away when ... the show got shut down.

We were out of time.

We had been given the whole exploding volcano speech, but didn't take into consideration that it put us really late into the evening, and the venue was only rented until a certain time. Some guy came rushing up to me from the side of the stage and said, "This is your last song! We're out of time, and the people from the Bren Center want us out of here!"

Screwed.

CHAPTER EIGHT

The band blasted through our last song, and the crowd seemed to release all of their energy, but I couldn't concentrate because my big chance to make some pre-excuses for myself had just disappeared. The crowd seemed to be only slightly bothered by the short set, because by that time everyone was so burned out they were ready to go do something else.

As the song ended, I pathetically attempted to shoot my speech out there anyway. Blind. Blind as a bat. (Forget the fact that the whole idea was ridiculous, selfish, and totally sinful in the first place.) I tried to get everyone's attention, tried to paint myself as some sort of fallen soldier in battle, and then something perfect happened.

Peace, Mr. Mischief, dumped a huge plastic cup of ice water on my head.

I stopped talking and immediately started to laugh ... and sort of cry. I had waited all day, all week, for my chance to prepare anyone and everyone that I could for what I was certain was coming ... and I couldn't. Denied. I was exhausted and a little delirious. I heard Peace shout into my ear, "Hey ... shut up! The show's over! C'mon, let's get out of here!"

The "woman time" came, and I was spared. (Depending on how you look at it, I guess. What kind of father could I have been? A better way to put it might be, "All were spared.") The only seed that was planted that day was a voice in the back of my head. It said, "This is all going to stop. You know it, and you need it."

Looking back on the lessons I refused to learn because I feared the actual pain of the lesson itself rather than the outcome, I get a little sad. So much could have been accomplished. Maybe. I don't know ... as a human, I sometimes can't help but wonder "what might have been." I know that God has His way, His sovereignty. I just don't know why or how it all plays out. I know where I am now, and I see that God had to teach me so many lessons the hard way. I know—for certain—I needed to learn them the way I did, or I would never have learned them at all. Second guessing myself now, of course I could have made everything easier on myself, humble obedience would have been a great place to start, but I only know that now because of what God has taught me since.

Sin has a way of blinding us ... partially. We see some of the truth, just enough to make ourselves feel better, but the reality—the direct offense to God—is usually something we simply don't want to see; it's hidden by the blinding power of sin. There really is no outsmarting our "Old Sin Nature." The Bible says, "The heart of man is desperately wicked, who can know it?" (Jeremiah 17:9). We can't outsmart our own wicked hearts ... plus, there is still the devil to deal with.

———————————— ❋ ————————————

When this fleeting limelight fades ...
and we're alone again
what name will your heart speak?
what is true? what is real?
not what you feel, what you know eternally
"I'm all right ..."
Ten years running blind and aimlessly
warming by the fires of bridges burning
Ten thousand peering eyes that can only see
the show, the smile, the face I allow
how many more break beneath the surface?
Young and bold, but blind, and led by blind
His person missed beyond His name
Was this the hope when we began?
A tragic generation

CHAPTER EIGHT

of faithless children and forgotten love?
I know I hoped for some other, higher purpose
If you see me on the way down
would you smile and send me on my way?
And if you see me headed down
is there something more between you and I?
Something Higher...

"BURNING CLEAN"
Stavesacre, *Friction*

For the final three years of the Crucified, I essentially led
two lives. With one life, I spent my Sundays and Tuesdays
at church, praying for forgiveness and searching the Scriptures for comfort from the alienation I felt. I knew what
the source of that alienation was—sin—but again, I refused
to turn away from it. With the other life, the active vehicle
for that sin, I did anything and everything I felt like doing.
I was a little bit like King Solomon in the first chapters of
Ecclesiastes ... without the greatness.

I became more and more uneasy with the praises I had
so willingly accepted before. I knew they were false, and I
had begun to realize that God was not going to let me just
continue on in sin—especially if I was aware of my sin. I
was living low, and yet every time we played, at least one or
two people would come up to me and tell me how much
the Holy Spirit could be seen in my life, or how much it
was apparent that I was a godly man. Every time I heard
something like that, I became more aware of my sin, and it
scared me. (I also developed a cynicism that I have yet to
shake completely. "Godly, eh? Sure about that?")

I experimented with the little drugs that came my way.
There wasn't much really, but what came around, I tried.
Even in my sin, I had no real desire to do drugs ... I still

feared them. I'm sure that fear saved me from an even more difficult road than the one I ended up taking, and I'm grateful for it, because when I think about what I've watched drugs do to friends of mine throughout the years, I can't measure the mercies God has shown on my behalf in sparing me from that little hell.

Once I lost my virginity, I just figured the battle I had tried to win my whole life was now a joke, so why try anymore? Here's something many of my friends have agreed with me on: It's a myth that men are the only ones who pursue casual sex. I think a lot of the Christians in the Church today, and maybe some old people, are the only souls on earth who still believe that. Being one of those mistaken people, I always expected women to continue ignoring me the way they did when I was younger. I was shocked when women actually noticed me. Of course, because of this new attention, I thought I was the king of the planet.

Oops.

The world is full of women who are just as shallow and easy as men. "If you put it out there, someone will pick it up." I didn't realize I was just another warm body until years later—after I had fooled myself into thinking that I was so much more. Realizing the truth was a cold splash of water.

And that was only one part of my rebellion. The person I became once I decided not to resist the temptations suddenly surrounding me was a real burden to the people who cared about me. I can only imagine what they must have been thinking as they watched me crawl further away from God, diving headfirst into a fantasy only I believed. I tried to hide the truth, but the only person who believed I was getting away with the lifestyle I was leading was me.

I turned into a selfish person who not only pushed away his God, but also his family and friends. I manipulated people to get my way. I told them what they wanted to hear to either take something from them or make them leave me alone. As the days went by, I lost friend after friend, and felt lonelier and lonelier.

Eventually I was found out, and no one wanted anything to do with me. I don't blame them either ... I wouldn't spend any time with a person who treated me the way I treated people back then. The Christians I knew had either turned their backs on me in condemnation, or had just given all they could give and had nothing left to offer but heartbreak—something I had no desire to acknowledge. Before I knew it, I was alone—there's something about lazy, selfish people that causes kind, generous ones to not come around much.

It was one thing to burn bridges with the Christians in my life. I could still do that and tell myself I was being persecuted or unfairly judged ... which, while sometimes true, was mostly just something I needed to believe to justify my life. It was another problem entirely to have the people in my life who were not Christians turn their backs on me. When that started to happen, I finally knew who I had become.

I could hate the Christians, but I had nothing to say to those who just thought I was a bad person. It's not persecution when you're just being a jerk. I had always tried to show people that not all Christians were judgmental or self-righteous. I always said, "You can't judge Jesus by the actions of His people." When I made statements like that, I always thought of the weird people with bullhorns on the sidewalks, or the televangelists of the world. I didn't realize self-righteousness could come in forms other than all of those easy targets. I never considered the possibility that people might just be sick and tired of fakes—and to their eyes, I was one. Unless you actually care about "struggles" or "backsliding," a person claiming to be a Christian and living like a devil is just one more reason not to hope. I never thought that maybe—probably—some people were just searching for something higher ... something true.

———————————⊛———————————

Because it's important in the larger scheme of things, I want to mention this:

I had been reading in Jeremiah about God's anger with the rebellion of His people. He warned them, He forgave them, He punished them, and He forgave them. Over and over, on and on—it went like this for years. They would right themselves one minute, then turn around and abandon Him in their hearts the next. I believed then, and still do now, that God was speaking to me through His Word as I read through those passages. (I don't know if I could prove that or base some doctrine on it, so please ... don't you do it either. I'm just saying what happened in my life; I don't know how God speaks to you in yours.) I had this feeling that He was talking to me.

I came to a part where essentially God said to His people, "If you continue on in the sins you are committing, I'm going to destroy everything you have built. Repent from your ways and return to Me." When that warning came down, it practically screamed out at me. I knew God was telling me to turn away from the sin in my life. I needed to acknowledge my sins, repent from them, and return to Him. Immediately.

So I did. For about ten minutes.

I obeyed long enough to forget the conviction I felt when I read that passage in Jeremiah. I cleaned up my act for a little while and then went right back into the same old sins—Samson style.

There was a girl, we'll call her Jane, who I had been

hanging around with. I had been trying to get together with her for a while, but the only way I could was to let her feel close to me. One night, I told her about what I had read in Jeremiah, and about how I was sure that God would take apart everything I (mistakenly) thought I had built. After a while, I forgot about what I told her.

Since I wasn't really interested in a relationship, I eventually hurt her feelings. Only mildly concerned, I came back around like a bad dog, whimpering and looking for some sympathy. It was the ol' "fallen soldier" angle—where I would sin and ask for forgiveness, then look for someone to sympathize with my weaknesses—and it was perfect for the ugly monster that I had turned into. I even started to feel sorry for myself ...

I said all the things she needed to hear, and I thought she bought my whole line. Jane seemed all too glad to forgive my previous faults, we slept together, and the relationship faded almost immediately—but I remember driving home that day thinking that I had just made a major mistake. It was as if all of what I had pushed out of my mind came flooding back in. Given the certainty I had felt after reading that passage in Jeremiah only a month or so earlier, I wondered if I had just taken a step that I wouldn't be able to take back. I pushed the fear back out of my head, and thought about something else.

HOW TO WEAR OUT YOUR WELCOME

After moving out of the apartment that Greg and I shared with Jeff and our friend Steve, we moved in with a young couple who were big fans of the band and had become friends with all of us. They opened their house to us with generosity and warmth, and we each moved into our own rooms, thinking we had it made. At first it was great. They bought us groceries, let us use the whole house, and basically treated us like family.

I had a job when I first moved in, but soon quit. I assumed that the band would be able to pay my bills and that my ... *ahem* ... solo album would be taking off any minute—so I would be making money off of all of the side opportunities that it created.

I had schemes left and right, all to try to make enough money to avoid working. A couple of friends invested in a "T-shirt company" called Pluto, and we put together some weak Christianized slogans, expecting to sell them at "such and such a profit, in such and such a city." I was certain that we would make great money, and I didn't even have to invest any of my own. Mark and his tendency toward manipulation strikes again.

Meanwhile, with money from their relatives, my roommates and I started a "clothing store" in Ragin' Records, our friend Paul's record shop. We expected to get all of the best brands and the hard-to-find labels that no one in the San Joaquin Valley had yet. We called it WorK Klothing, and even tried to make some of our own designs to sell at trade shows, in the store, and through the mail—hoping for some of the success the Crucified had through mail order.

All of these ideas were okay, I just expected them all to automatically do as well as the Crucified's various endeavors had. Sell that name, right?

Wrong.

PLUTO: FARTHER AWAY THAN YOU THINK

We sold the Pluto T-shirts at the festival that had been an automatic money tree for the Crucified—Cornerstone—and did all right ... then I spent most of the money before I even got home. I just told myself that I would be able to sell some more shirts later! I had no self-discipline to speak of, and yet I expected to have self-control ... once again: Oops.

By the time I got back from the festival, I had just enough money (well ... almost) to cover one of the friends who had invested in Pluto, a Christian friend who had been close to me all through high school. I had the money in my wallet, where it was nearly impossible to make sure it remained, and stopped at a park to hang out with a girl I had my eye on. I sat on a bench made of concrete, and the wallet, full of twenties, was uncomfortable in my pocket. I took it out and set it next to me on the bench. I was so caught up in talking to this girl that I just forgot it there.

Now I had to come up with the money for my friend find money to live off of—all without a job and nothing to fall back on.

It would have been one thing to hand the guy some, if not all, of the money he had invested, then tell him the rest was on the way. It was something else completely to say I had nothing at all to give. I paid him off—much later—but it was such a bad experience that we never messed with the idea again. The remaining shirts stayed in a box in my garage, until about five or six years later, when I donated them to the Salvation Army. A total waste.

The other partner in the deal, whose mother put up some of the money to get the whole thing started, got nothing. I wormed my way out of telling him much, and then he never really came around again. I was actually so self-consumed that I thought of it as a relief, because he was one more person I didn't have to face anymore. This was a tragedy. He was a good friend, something I have since grown—thank God—to value higher than gold, but in that case, I was too late. I lost his friendship and haven't seen him in years. He cared for me, and got screwed for it.

He also wasn't a Christian. Now, what do you think goes through his mind when someone says not to blame Jesus for the way His people act?

WORK ... AND IRONY

The "clothing store" was a disaster. We tried to do it right: We had no overhead past our initial buy, and we knew where to go to meet all of the people who could help us get the clothes we wanted. We became friends with a girl who worked for a successful underground clothing label in southern California, and she tried to hook us up with whatever she could, but soon grew weary of carrying us. In the end, no one but her and a few easily accessible labels would sell to us.

You want an industry that a punk rocker was never going to fit into? Try: Snobby Fashion.

Aside from the very few people who were like our friend in L.A., most of the people in the pseudo-underground retail business—cool labels and exclusive brands—were complete jerks. They wouldn't return calls for anything, and if you met with them and they determined you weren't immediately going to boost the image of their label, they would treat you like garbage. Some companies would leave you hanging for weeks, then send you clothes you didn't order—usually what they couldn't sell elsewhere. It was a total drag.

We went to the huge ASR Convention—a convention where it is very likely that every label of clothing you are wearing right this moment sends a representative to net-work with other labels and retail buyers—and nearly had the stuffing kicked out of us. We walked through the convention with our "WorK Klothing" business cards and our one T-shirt design and got exactly no love from any of the other brands that we tried to carry. It was like being invited to a private party and showing up early, only to find that everyone there hated our guts and wasn't going to show up until we left. Yeah, lots of fun. We couldn't attract any attention from the brands that we thought were going to make our store a success, and we died with clothes that became old news in a matter of months.

Who got stuck with the clothes we initially bought? Oh, you weren't going to say me, were you? No, hard as it may be to believe, I mostly left my roommates twisting in the wind. I wouldn't even go down to the store anymore—my favorite record store in the world! No way, my pride was stinging too hard. Paul, one of my closest friends, practically gave me the perfect opportunity to start something legitimate—and had I invested more than vanity in it, I might have done well. But it was no good. I was too prideful and too lazy, and my roommates (no, my landlords ... my friends) were left trying to scramble with the broken pieces.

I know, I hate me right now, too.

The Crucified played the big shows and had the high expectations, but we didn't have the peace of mind that is supposed to come with that sort of thing. In addition to the growing fear in the back of my mind as to what was going to happen to me, there was a steady uneasiness about the band itself. These days, when Stavesacre is out on the road, or just hanging out around each other, for the most part, we have a good time. Even with the weird quirks and idiosyncrasies of each of our members, we still like each other. I would never hesitate to hang out with anyone from Stavesacre outside of something directly related to the band. That's just how we are, and to be fair, that was one of the elements we knew to look for when the band started out. The Crucified was a different matter. Sure, we liked each other, at least enough to not hate each other ... but that was about it. There were very strange dynamics to our friendships within the band, and those dynamics often made themselves apparent.

Having said that, I will now disappoint any dirty laundry collectors by not going into any specifics—who did this, who was always doing that, etc. As most bands worth being called bands would say, "What happens in the van, stays in the van." It's about unity, loyalty, and family—even now. Needless to say, there was a lot of tension, a lot of hurt feelings that had been building up for years, and a lot of unfinished business that didn't look like it would get finished any time soon. We had no money and little to look forward to. Our label had no idea what was going on in the music world around us, and really no idea what to do with us in the first place. There were big talks with big players in the business, but they always ended up in postponed meetings, missed shows, and phone tag.

All of the problems we had individually came to the surface together. Each of us was going through our own moments of truth. I wasn't the only person who was running from the Lord—in our own way, I think each of us was.

There was no real excitement for the band, the new music was crawling along, and everyone was ready for some kind of change. We were trying to look on the bright side, but there wasn't much of one left to look at.

DON'T WALK, RUN

Obviously, I was going downhill in almost every direction. My roommates informed me that I needed to move out—it wasn't just the store, it was the way I took them and their home for granted. I couldn't go live with the band members because we were all mostly tolerating each other at that point anyway. My parents and I were still completely locked in combat, so I couldn't go home. All of the bridges I might have been able to cross back over before were completely burned out.

I needed to find somewhere to go, and no one was going to open up a door for me. I had to wake up and do something right. I knew this wasn't just a window for me to salvage my own dignity, it was probably the last time I would have a chance to take some responsibility for my own life. Besides, I didn't really have a choice.

The Crucified's manager lived in southern California, in the San Fernando Valley, and his wife was the manager of a big apartment complex in Woodland Hills. He told me that she could help me get my own place. He also had a friend who owned his own plumbing business, and he told me the guy was looking for some help. That sounded like the best idea I had heard in a long time, so I told my manager to have his wife start looking for an empty one-bedroom. With nowhere else to go, I picked up all I had, put it into the back of my truck, and moved to Woodland Hills.

The plan was to move down south, make some money, and commute to Fresno the way Bellew had when he first joined the band. I would supposedly be making a lot of cash, so in theory, moving down south would be easier on everyone. My manager would keep the show going, and everything would be wonderful.

Just wonderful.

I called my parents and told them I needed to see them, so I went over to their new house. By this time, they had sold the house out in Madera Ranchos and moved into Fresno to be closer to their church. They were always driving into town, and now they lived right down the street from their pastor and only a few minutes from the church building. It was sad for me. I had grown to love that house in the country, but with no more kids going to school, it made more sense for my parents to live in Fresno. Something about their move made it both easier and more difficult to tell them I was leaving. Their new house held no fond memories for me, but leaving my parents from an unfamiliar place further accentuated my feelings of alienation.

I told them as much of the truth about where my life had gone as I could. I explained that I needed to get out of town and to be forced to take care of myself, and that was it.

That night, I left Fresno, but first I stopped by a club to see some friends from a local punk/funk band who were playing a show there. A couple of the guys had played on the Native Son album, and a lot of my other friends were going to be there. I had all of my possessions in the back of my truck and was ready to go. I watched the show, said some goodbyes, and hopped back into my truck to leave.

One of the guys from the band came up to my truck and tapped on the window. We had worked together at one of my many jobs and had also gone to a couple shows together ... I guess I'd say we were friends. I remember rolling down my window to talk to him, assuming that he was coming to say goodbye to me. I started to say goodbye myself when he cut me off.

"Hey Mark. So you're leaving tonight, eh? Wow, have a safe trip. Yeah, I just wanted to tell you that all of that time we worked together, I really thought you were different from everyone else I knew. Out of all the people I've met who called themselves Christians, you were one person who actually backed it up, and I always thought that was cool ... it gave me some hope."

I sat, beaming with pride, in my truck. As I reached out to shake hands with him, he shook his head, and left his hand hanging by his side.

"Yeah, I just wanted to let you know how disappointed I was to find out that all of that was bullsh--. I know what you've been doing. I know you what you did with _____, and I think that sucks. She's my girlfriend now, but she still talks about you. I can't believe you would do that." He shook his head again.

"Have a nice life." He turned and walked away.

CHAPTER EIGHT

One more chicken coming back home to roost. The whole situation was so symbolic I could barely stand it. I sat in my truck with my mouth open. I didn't cry, I didn't beg for forgiveness, I just turned the key and got out of there.

There is no real benefit to going into much more detail regarding those years. They were hard, and I was so lonely that even coming back to them in memory is difficult to do.

I had only me to blame, and I couldn't shake that realization. I was sad because I missed my fellowship with God, and fellowship with the people that I knew really loved me, and I knew those breaks in fellowship were my fault.

THE GAP

One of the ironic things about music is the relationship between the fans and the artists. There is a huge gap of understanding that exists between those two groups of people. I believe it shows itself most consistently to the artists—you write a song, you put it out, and then you wait to see if anyone in the world is going to relate to it. (Of course there are exceptions, some songs are so straight forward there can really be no misunderstanding between the writer and the listener. Unfortunately, those songs are often about as interesting and enriching to the soul as fast food is to the body.) For most people who are trying to write songs or be creative in some new and refreshing way, there is a gap between what the artist is saying and what the fan is hearing. That's not necessarily bad, in fact I think its part of what makes art ... art. It can enrich a fan's life to be exposed to it, and it can enrich an artist's life to let their creativity out—both aspects bounce off of each other and everybody gets something out of it.

The irony becomes painful though, when the gap between the artist and the fan takes a personal angle, particularly one that involves right and wrong, good and evil, and beliefs that extend beyond opinion and into faith. (And yes, if you hadn't figured it out by now, I do believe there is a distinction between faith and opinion. Faith often challenges and even changes opinion.) That gap then becomes more personal than an artistic relationship generally is, and it creates its own strange dynamics.

All of my drama came to a head when the Crucified was at its peak, and the gap got me. We were still very close with our fans and wanted to be approachable—punk rock was still the source of so much for us that we probably would never be free from the secret fear of appearing as "rock stars"—so we were always around somebody with a question about a song or an opinion about something we said. It still amazes me how far off some people can be from the truth behind a lyric or a statement. (One misconstrued lyric and a couple hours of developing an opinion around that lyric, and a song about breaking up with your girlfriend becomes an anthem about turning your back on God.) While the Crucified's lyrics were, as a rule, straightforward—Stavesacre would have all sorts of trouble with the lyrical-content issue later—the leap in logic the fans took with us still played a major role in my life, although it was more about lifestyle than lyrics.

The assumption, aside from the usual "Hey, you have an album out, you must be rich" misconception, was that the Crucified were all incredibly godly people. That was obviously not the truth about me, but the point isn't that we were sinners—that's not news—but that when a constant stream of people come around telling you strange things like, "The Spirit of God was sooo there tonight!" or "Oh ... I can tell that you guys are just totally anointed!" and you are still worried about your pregnant girlfriend, you feel like a liar. I would hear those types of comments all the time and try to dismiss them with a contrary statement, and people would just assume I was being humble.

Argh!!

We would get so much credit for things that God was doing in spite of us, and then when we tried to separate ourselves from that improper credit, people would think we were all the more godly for being modest!

After a while, I just started to feel like such a fraud … there had been times when I presented myself as this great Christian, when in fact, I was a manipulative person, a bad friend, and a womanizing slut. I might be able to convince myself that my shortcomings were just "difficulties" or "struggles." Then I would be at a show and have some kid tell me about how God was totally using me, how I was ob- viously close to Him, etc., and the truth would scream out at me. I existed in a steady conflict of error, where I felt like a hypocrite—sometimes whether I was conscious of my sin or not—and after a while, I just felt alone. The gap sucks.

Another dynamic of it is that it breeds the cynicism I mentioned earlier. After so many people have made such far-reaching comments as "God is evident in your life," or "God totally ministered to me through the things you said tonight/things you wrote in your song/way you live/carry yourself," you start to see that mostly they just want to say them. You learn that they want to believe them, and that leads to wanting to learn why they want to believe them. It also gives a whole new twist to these things when you know they aren't true—you can't help but feel like a fraud … or like the person saying them is one. And what are the implications on a grander scale, one that includes pastors and whole churches? If you start thinking about it too much, pretty soon everyone looks desperate to believe in anything. You have to remind yourself of what you know to be true on a daily basis, just to keep some perspective.

I never wondered whether or not God was really true,

but I sure did wonder if it mattered whether or not I was. I figured that these people were going to believe what they wanted to, but I knew that sooner or later, the truth would come out, and I wouldn't only feel sorrow for my sins, I would also feel like a disappointment and a disgrace.

I think I began to retreat into my cocoon right about the time I started to realize all of this, and somewhere in the back of my mind, I knew that I was about to be a very lonely person.

THE SWEET SMELL OF HUMILITY

Shortly after I moved down to the San Fernando Valley, everything came to a close.

The plumbing apprenticeship was a joke. My manager's friend with the business left me hanging, didn't return phone calls, and the few times I saw him after I'd moved down, seemed to have forgotten the whole idea entirely. For the first month I was down there, I slept on my manager's floor while I waited for an apartment to open up. Since the apprenticeship didn't look too promising, I needed to find a job of some kind, and ended up on the apartment complex remodeling crew. My big plan for a plumbing career turned out to be not so much a plumbing career as it was a paintscraping/wall-cleaning/stair-sweeping one. I spent my days plastering over stress damage in the walls and putting sealing caulk on windowsills that were coming undone. (My favorite gig during my stint on the "remodeling crew" was spraying a high-pressure washer—a super-powered squirt gun—on every inch of the complex's carport walls and ceilings. It was a three-story, three-hundred-plus tenant building. I stood in puddles of water for anywhere from eight to twelve hours a day for three days. All of the calluses on my feet came off. I never once stopped thinking: I'VE REALLY MADE IT NOW.)

I commuted to Fresno for the first couple of weeks and

tried to keep the dream alive, but something was wrong, and everybody knew it. Something felt ... desperate. The first weekend after I moved, the Crucified played another huge show in Laguna Beach at Club Post Nuclear. Some big-time record company guy who Ocean had introduced us to, who we'll call Eddie, was supposed to show up. Our manager and I met with him earlier during the week of the show and talked about the potential of the band, our consistently growing shows, and how we "might be onto something big." Our conversation with him ended with us asking if he would be at the show the coming weekend, and he replied, "I don't see how I could miss it. I'm not looking to be your friend, and I'm not even really into the music. I'm interested in the business potential of this band, and I can see there is something going on here. Once I talk to your record label again, I think we could have a lot of fun making money together."

The show came; Eddie did not. We never heard from him again. When he didn't show up, there was almost an audible snap in the air. That snap was our last thread of expectation. Once he disappeared—our best bet at "making it" with the band—everyone seemed to lose their will. All the secrets that had been hidden in the dark were immediately brought to light, and everyone came clean about what was going on in their personal lives. One of the guys quit, and we were left looking for a replacement. It seemed that with no big payday coming, there was little room for patience, hope, or expectation.

We started looking for a new member right away—our manager was really freaking out, with our biggest tour to-date booked, and only a month or so away—and we thought we had found one. After practicing with the new guy for about two weeks, I knew it wasn't going to work out. Too big of a change had taken place—more than just a lost band member—and there wasn't enough excitement to make adding another new personality worth all of the work. We all tried not to notice.

After a month of sleeping on the floor, a one-bedroom apartment finally opened up. By the end of that first month, my manager's wife, now my landlord, was clearly tired of having me around their apartment and did little to disguise it. She started acting weird, even mean, and my manager just sort of did nothing and never talked to me. I was glad to be moving out—I felt like I had just started over where I left off up in Fresno. Even after I moved out, two doors down from them, they basically pretended I was a stranger—sometimes bolting the door when I knocked, then opening it just enough to peek out and ask, "WHO IS IT?"

That was it for me. I no longer *felt* totally alone, I *was* alone. Good-bye last friend on earth.

One day, rather conveniently a payday, my boss just didn't show up, and everyone on the crew quit. I was the only guy who spoke English, so no one could explain to me what was going on. I just stood around waiting for my assignment for the day, while all of the guys cursed in Spanish and gathered their tools. I eventually got enough information to realize that I no longer had employment.

I had no job, no credit, no television … and no friends.

I went looking for work, trying the malls and the paper. There wasn't much available, but it wouldn't have mattered if there was: I think I was blind to any good opportunities that might have come my way. I believe that God allowed me to have total control of my life, and to be left to my own decisions. I also believe He allowed this to happen to show me how much I needed Him, and how much He had given me. I had experience waiting tables, even working room service in hotels, but I never even thought to fall back on that. I was still looking for something I could do on the side and not have to change my appearance, and remain able to walk away as soon as something happened for me in music. It was ridiculous.

I also think God separated me from all of the people who
loved me despite my shortcomings, because He wanted
to teach me total dependence on Him. There were some
people who still came around, who still called and asked
me out, but their presence actually seemed to further my
feelings of loneliness. (My truck broke down about four
months after I moved into the apartment, and some old
friends loaned me a car. It was a total blessing, but other
than work, I had nowhere else to go. Knowing there was a
car out in the parking lot available for me to drive made the
reality of having nowhere to go that much more painful. I
mostly drove it to their house to hang out with them.) I felt
like a person living in a foreign country who kept bumping
into tourists from back home who couldn't stay long.

I eventually got a terrible job—washing windows, which
I also had experience doing—making just enough to pay
my bills. Almost. I worked six days a week, from seven in
the morning until four or five at night, and essentially shut
myself off from the rest of the world.

THE END

On a hot San Fernando Valley summer day in 1993, I
drove home from work with no A/C, no automatic trans-
mission, and no joy. After eight hours of climbing through
bushes, hanging off ladders, and scraping spiders off of my
face, I tackled rush hour traffic the way I did every day.
When I pulled off of the 118 freeway, my truck stalled on
Topanga Canyon Road, one of the busiest streets in the
Valley. I pushed it four or five blocks, stopping at the lights,
trying to find a place where I could park and avoid being
towed.

I walked the rest of the way, about a mile and a half, back
to my empty one-bedroom "home." (I clearly remember
that while walking down the street, it seemed like every car

that passed me had "Ain't Nothin' But a G Thing" blasting out of the windows.) I got some Taco Bell and turned the last corner to my house. The sun had started to set into the smog by the time I made that turn, and the sky looked beautiful: twisting reds and oranges, thin wisps of cloud, and the hills just above the Valley on the horizon.

When I came inside, there were two messages on my phone. The first was Jim, our drummer. He called and left a message that stabbed me through the ear.

"Hey man, it's Jim. Look, we need to talk. Well ... just call me back."

I sat down. I didn't need to call Jim to ask him what was up; I already knew.

The other message was the sound of the operator— someone had called and hung up, but my lousy answering machine always held the line open. The message was a recorded voice that said, over and over, "If you'd like to make a call, please hang up and try again. Beep! If you'd like to make a call ..."

And so ... the Crucified broke up. I talked to Jim, and he said what we had both been thinking, maybe even fearing.

No. That's not true. I was afraid.

On the phone, I told Jim that the band was all I knew how to do. I was devastated, but only because I felt like everything—my personal life, my spiritual life, and my professional life—had piled up nice and high, and then fell on me. It was the finality of it all that was shocking. Even Jim's comforting words drove the point home further: This is over. No more trying, no more next record. The music that we had written was empty anyway, with the bits of it that were decent better served by not being used at all. The lackluster passion they would have received from us would have done them no justice. (I think some of the better ideas did get the attention they deserved when Jeff did his solo album, *CHATTERbOX*.) I was certain I would now finish out my existence in anonymity—"Unwept, unheard, and unsung" (Sir Walter Scott ... by way of Bill Murray's *Groundhog Day*). That reads a little too dramatic now, but only because the reality of how I felt then has faded over the years.

Out of respect for the individual members of the band, the details involving the Crucified's breakup will remain private, as I mentioned before. Doesn't matter much anyway. We canceled all of our summer tour dates—a tour that would have been our biggest and most legitimate—much to the displeasure of some hardworking, nice people who invested a lot of their time and money. My manager made a weak attempt at getting me to do the dates with a make-up band, but I wanted nothing to do with it. Our relationship, which had already been on the backburner for some time, completely dissolved.

Native Son eventually became so wearisome that I put it behind me for good, and that was that.

Music was the one thing that I had ever truly worked hard at. I put my passion into it, I took risks, and I loved being a part of it. By my own doing, I was now faced with the possibility of never being a part of it again. God finally did have to take away something precious to me. To get my attention back, to get me to follow Him, He had to show me that what started out as something good, what at one point was a blessing from Him, had now become just another offering at the throne of my heart—where He no longer sat. I had replaced Him with my pride.

Hey, at the time, it was all that I knew, it was all that I had built. I guess what was most difficult about knowing that I wasn't going to get my way was knowing that loss was what

I deserved. I deserved to be disappointed; I deserved to be denied.

I spent the majority of that summer alone in my house. I worked all day long, came home, and fell asleep in the shower, or on my bed in my room. I would wake up hours later, or sometimes the next morning. On the nights that I woke up in the small hours, when it felt like the whole world was still sleeping, I would walk all around town, trying to make myself tired again. Sometimes I would spend my nights up on the rooftops of my apartment complex, looking at the stars and the lights of the city and wondering what was going to happen to me. I sometimes wondered what would happen if I fell off ... or made myself fall off. (Who would notice?)

I prayed a lot, and I believe that during some of those nights, God spoke to me in the still small voice that I had heard about my whole life. He told me that He was humbling me, and that He was saving me.

Still to this day, I am tempted by the lifestyle I allowed myself to be a part of, and that has also taught me a lesson: Some memories don't fade. They come back to haunt you like ghosts, and I believe that if it doesn't take dying, it's going to take a whole lot of living for some of those ghosts to stop knocking on my door in the middle of the night ...

A careless leper,
too comfortable in his own world
to notice the older wounds ...
had new infections
with new intentions
Darkness settled in behind me

CHAPTER EIGHT

tapped me on the shoulder
singing shivers to my spine
from the corners of my mind,
"I've been wanting to remind you
of everything you've left behind ...
and wouldn't you, shouldn't you remember me?
Should you forget, I haven't yet
Remember when we almost stepped right off
between the two heavens?
One above and one below
One last flight, all stars and city lights
One last goodbye ..."
She's there when I'm alone and she always seems
to know
the stories that will take me
back to where my comforts sleep
A caress with velvet paws
that hide her sharpened claws
Along the walls that time has built high
searching for the blemishes
And I know she's breathing murder
that it is folly to endure her
but there is sweetness in her whispers
"When you've had enough, I'll be waiting
Wouldn't you, shouldn't you remember me?
Should you forget, I haven't yet ...
you know that we could always
step right off ..."

"THE TWO HEAVENS"
Stavesacre, *Absolutes*

———————————❂———————————

That time of my life has always reminded me of a story
I read when I was a kid. The story was from part of *The*

Chronicles of Narnia, by C.S. Lewis. I believe it came from the book *Voyage of the Dawn Treader*. Please, allow me to loosely paraphrase:

There was a little boy named Eustace Clarence Scrubb, who was a spoiled brat. He was traveling on a boat, the Dawn Treader, with his cousins and his friends, and they stopped on an island. Eustace wandered off by himself and discovered a cave filled with treasure. He decided he wouldn't tell anyone about the treasure. That night, he slept in the cave, but before he went to sleep, he put on a gold bracelet. When he woke up the next morning, he had turned into a dragon. He noticed the change first because he had an incredible pain in his arm. He looked down and saw that he had turned into a dragon, but that his clothing and bracelet had remained the same size. Eustace cried out for help, and Aslan the Lion eventually came to his aid. Aslan told Eustace that he could help him, but it would hurt. Eustace replied that any pain would be better than the pain he was going through at that moment, and so Aslan agreed to help him. First he led Eustace to a well and told him to undress, bathe, and peel off some of his skin. Then, using his giant lion's claws, he peeled off the remaining layers of scales that covered the boy. Layer by layer, he removed the dragon's skin that covered Eustace, and eventually he was freed from the pain of the bracelet. It was agonizing, but it was a necessary process to ultimately release the boy from his own self-inflicted bondage.

Yes, in that still small voice, I do believe that God was telling me He was humbling me, but I also believe that He was reminding me that He loved me, and that's what brought me back.

I had no "white light experience"; I didn't see a vision. I had many layers of "dragon's skin," and it took some time. But I knew that if I let go of the sin I had been trying to hold on to, He would let me feel good again. It was His faithfulness that spoke to me in those times, and it was the gentle grace He has always shown me that brought me back to Him.

"At every turn she's there ..."

NINE

HOW TO LOSE HOPE

There is a little pizza joint/club in Little Rock, Arkansas called Vino's. Stavesacre have played there quite a few times, but one show stands out in my memory, more so than just about any show we've ever played. We were on tour, I think the first of many supporting *Speakeasy*, and we were all pretty happy to be playing Vino's because, while they aren't really known for great shows, their pizza is good, and they keep the beverages flowing. It's nice. We have some old friends there in Little Rock, and that's always nice as well—seeing familiar faces on the road is never bad.

We were sitting in the club talking and catching up, selling merchandise and sort of hanging with the fans. A tall young man approached me and asked me to step aside with him because he "had something important to talk to me about."

(Spidey Senses Tingling)

That's the usual opening line when someone has something to share that they have decided is "from the Lord."

CHAPTER NINE

And, as usual, I responded with "right now is not the time," maybe he could write me, etc. He insisted, saying that what he had to tell me was urgent, and then dropped the big one: What he had to tell me was "from the Lord." Not surprised.

This usually gets a would-be assailant the same response as any other: dismissal. If it seems the person's feelings are hurt, I often include an explanation as to why I like to keep relationships with fans fairly impersonal, as I simply do not have the emotional resources to accommodate extremely heavy interpersonal communication with someone who is—"no disrespect intended"—a total stranger. But then things changed, and he said something that actually got my attention.

"It's about your sister."

Shock.

I have been as frank and as personal in this book as possible, because I can control this forum. That control is not a contradiction, because in this forum, I have the luxury of explaining myself in context with my personal life, and I can state the fullness of my thinking, my perspective, and my experience in a way that is appropriate. But (it sucks that I should even have to say this, but I do) don't expect me to talk about this story the next time you see me. Once you have truly read the book, if you comprehend anything I have been saying, you will realize what is appropriate for discussion and what is not.

For all of you who still don't see where I'm going with this: This is a topic that I don't want to talk about. And I especially don't want to discuss it as small talk at a show or some other casual setting. Cool? Cool.

At the time this young man approached me, my sister had just recently given birth to her second and final child, my niece. She was born with a rare disease, one that caused her a lot of problems while she was still in the womb. She was born with a hole in her heart, and her stomach would not digest food, and in addition to many other difficulties, these things were not known until her birth. The doctors said they didn't expect her to live long, but my sister was intent on giving her the best life possible with the short time she had.

This was a difficult time for our family, and my sister was on my mind quite often. All of the questions she could be asking herself, all of the cross-examining she could be putting herself through ... I had no words to say for her, and I certainly had no answers for any of those questions, whatever they might have been. When this person came to me, telling me he had a message for me "from God," and about my sister no less, the part of me that still believes people are sincere—and that miracles do still happen—wanted to know what he had to say.

When he approached me and stated that he had a message from God for me about my sister, my response was this:

"Okay, look. I don't normally even listen to anyone who starts their conversations like you just did, but what you said makes me want to hear you out, even if I can't really bring myself to trust a total stranger with something this personal. Who knows? Maybe God's gonna say something to me that I need to hear ... I don't know."

The young man nodded in agreement, slow and steady, still with the too-grim and overly sincere look on his face. I ignored that little voice, the Spidey Senses, and kept on.

"So, I'll tell you what. You come and meet me at the van after the show is over. If you have something to tell me, you can tell it to me then."

We played, sold our merchandise, loaded out our gear, and got ready to leave. Outside at the van, the young man met me. I warned him that if he was going to tell me something he was claiming God had told him to tell me,

CHAPTER NINE

he better be right—because according to His Word, as far as I understood, God doesn't like to be falsely represented. I mean, I don't exactly know what a prophet is, but I do know I don't want to be a false one.

He said to me, "Ask me whatever you want to know about your sister. God wants to give you an answer, and that's why I'm here."

Without hesitation, I asked him, "Is my sister's newborn baby going to be all right, or will she die from the disease she has—"

He cut me off, "She will be healed of everything."

I paused.

"Oh yeah?" I asked.

He nodded, again with the same face he approached me with.

I told him, "Okay then. The next time we play through here, you better be here. Because if what you say is true, you should want to know. And if what you say is incorrect, then you should know you're in danger of being a false prophet. All right? Good. See you next time we come through."

And that was it.

Four months later, God used the passing of my niece to bring my family closer than we have been since I was a kid. It was one of the hardest experiences we've ever gone through together, but it was beautiful in its own way. Kyra Lily was part of our lives and then she wasn't, but in the short time she was, God used her mightily.

I've played Vino's two or three times since my encounter with that young man. I haven't seen him since our first conversation. I suppose he could be scared, maybe he even goes through some huge crisis of faith every time we come to town—asking himself if he has the faith to find out what happened to my niece, or the courage to face the possibility he might have been mistaken. Maybe he has made himself feel better by blaming the possibility that my niece died on my lack of faith, or a lack of faith on my sister's part ... who knows? I just wonder sometimes.

Do I think he's a false prophet? You know ... I don't know. I don't really care. I do know that I don't have the energy to have these kinds of experiences forever. I know people, not just me, shouldn't be put into situations where other people, who don't understand the real effect of their words, can just spill them out, unchecked and unaccountable, all over anyone around. I don't wish the seven plagues on the guy—he is just a kid, though one who is seriously misinformed—but I do want him, and people like him, to stay away from me.

———————————⊛———————————

Sometimes, I find myself believing I can change all of this. I find myself thinking that if I just have the right response prepared, then maybe the person to whom I am speaking will suddenly ... "get it." I wonder what life would be like if I could somehow steer my brothers and sisters away from inflicting these kinds of accidental wounds. I think that would be something worth living for.

BALMER'S EPIPHANY
Nowhere, Nebraska. (Or someplace just like it.)

While on tour, Stavesacre met up with a band called Plankeye to play a show way out in the middle of nowhere. When we entered the city limits (population twenty-five-hundred-ish), we could tell the show was going to be rough. How well can you expect a show to do when it would take attendance by at least a fifth of the town's population to fill the venue?

The day's drive there had been a scenic one: Plenty of the beautiful open plains of America's heartland, wonderfully accented by huge thunderclouds and quite an electrical storm.

We arrived at the venue, a church, to find a flatbed trailer behind the building and a dirt field. (Well, a mud field—it had been raining off and on for the last day or so.) The church property was up on a hill, and the wind was really kicking. The sound system, though not a bad one, was covered in plastic. A large plastic sheet was duct-taped to the soundboard, and two others covered the speakers on either side of the stage. As we began to load our gear inside the church, a few ominous drops of water landed here and there. Somewhere off in the background, you could hear statements like, "It might rain, make sure that plastic is taped down right!"

The stage (enter flat-bed trailer) had a temporary riser made up of some boxes and sheets of plywood. The bands were to set up on the trailer; the crowd was to stand in the mud. To keep the masses of swarming fans—about twenty kids wearing various band sweatshirts who were huddling together in one corner of the field—under control, there were plenty of security guards with jackets that said, surprise, SECURITY, on the back.

Both bands sat inside after eating the pre-show meal, glad for the chance to sit with familiar faces and catch up. After sharing some comical tales of woe from our respective tours, the attention of our conversation turned to the night's show, and the likelihood of at least one of us meeting our doom right here in the windy, rainy Nebraskan wastelands—during the gig. Who might be electrocuted by a microphone or guitar amp? Who would be the first to take a wrong turn while on the "stage" and end up with a compound fracture?

When we had finished our meals, Eric Balmer of Plank-eye noticed a nearly empty bottle of ranch dressing that was still sitting on the table. He picked it up and said:

"You know, tours like this ... it's like: The ranch dressing in this bottle represents all of my artistic dignity and integrity. The shows are a lot like a salad made up of nothing but lettuce. At first, it's nothing to spread it all over the lettuce; there's plenty to go around. But as you go along, you start to run out. It's no longer enough to just play, because these shows are so ridiculous that after a while, you've spread the dressing so thin that you're forced to add water to it just to keep it going. Pretty soon, all you have is cloudy water and lots of lettuce."

We laughed, a lot. The knowing kind of laughter that comes from a perfectly understood joke.

Oh yeah, no one was electrocuted. Or had compound fractures.

CHAPTER NINE

TEN

WHERE IT CAME BACK TO LIFE

By the end of the summer of '93, about five months after the Crucified broke up, I think God decided I had been alone for long enough. I wasn't looking for a band or some woman to make me feel better; I just wanted to be happy again, and I wanted to be and feel close to Him. Sure, I still struggled with pride and sin issues, but not like before. I had given my heart back to Jesus, and now I wanted to be around some people who would help me leave it there. I didn't want to be around someone so that I could take something from them. For the first time in a long time, I wanted to give, and I wanted to share. The time for learning on my own was over, and now I needed to learn how to be around people. I didn't want someone to hold my hand or keep me from falling; I just wanted to be around people who could help me be a better person, and if I could some- how help those same people, I would.

It was interesting the way my situation turned around. Some of what I remember:

An old friend, Tim Mann, the singer of Focused, bumped

into me at a show Peace managed to drag me to, down in Orange County. As I remember, I didn't want to go, but Peace insisted, and eventually I went along. Tim told me at the show that he and a bunch of other Christian guys were living in a big, three-bedroom apartment in Huntington Beach, and that they needed a roommate. He asked if I knew of anyone who might need a place to stay, and I actually said, "Oh. I don't know."

!

I was so out of it, I didn't even think that maybe I could move in there. Here was the fellowship and the company I was in need of, and it didn't even occur to me.

I went home that night, and while I was lying on my bed, the thought just popped into my head.

I could just leave this place. Right now.

The following afternoon, I called Tim about the room and asked if I could move in. He said yes, and that he'd have it ready and waiting for me whenever I wanted to come down. I broke my lease that day. I went into my landlord's office, where my ex-manager's wife sat doing whatever it was that she did, and told her I was leaving. I told her the truth, that I was broke and lonely, and I needed to get out of there. She just stared at me and said, "Go then, but you're breaking your lease. They'll want their money, and they'll get it. So go, I'll rent the room out soon enough." She then sat back in her chair and smiled. I told her I didn't care, and then I walked out the door and never saw her again.

I did speak to my old manager though. And it was strange. Shortly after I moved away, he became his old, friendly self again—further evidence to support my theory that God intended for me to be shut off from the rest of the world for a season.

I moved in September of 1993. I went from living in the hot San Fernando Valley all by myself with no friends to living in a place with six Christian roommates and a ten-minute bike ride to the beach. It was an unbelievable change and one of the happiest times of my life.

ALL IN ITS PROPER PLACE

When I moved into my room (which I had all to myself in a house with six guys already living there—incredible) I was shy and reserved. I think my new roommates, many of whom had played in bands that opened for the Crucified during our run, were a little put off at first. They probably expected me to act like I was some kind of star, so when I didn't talk to them much right away, their fears seemed confirmed. I was oblivious to this, because I just didn't know how to relate to anybody at the time. I was still coming out of my strange season in hell, and I was also really embarrassed at the state in which I arrived. I felt like they were doing me a favor—and they were—and I just didn't want to get in their way or be a burden. I mean, when I arrived at the house, I literally coasted in. I had no money, and no gas, and I was driving a borrowed car that I had to return. I needed a loan from my roommates—many of whom were total strangers—just to get back to the Valley to pick up my truck, which had broken down a month before I moved. (I managed to get my truck to wobble down to Huntington, only to leave it parked for six months in the one parking spot allotted to our apartment.) It was humiliating. Of course, I still had some pride issues, but due to my circumstances, each day seemed to put those issues more and more in check.

The week I moved in, I came down with the flu. I had no money and no transportation and needed to work badly, but finding a way up to the Valley to wash windows wouldn't have done any good anyway, because I was too sick to work. I spent the first day I was sick in my room. The second day, two of my roommates knocked on my door and asked if I was okay. I told them yeah, I was just sick, etc. I didn't want them to notice me as it was, much less feel sorry for me. A few minutes later, they knocked on my door and asked if they could come in. This time when I answered yes, they came into the room carrying orange juice and hot soup. They took care of me and were honestly concerned. I was blown away. On the third day I was sick, I came out of my room and got to know them. Lesson learned.

I was meant to be there. I began to learn again, and I began to grow again. This isn't a movie—I've had many hard times and made plenty of bad choices since those first days of living in Orange County—but I will always believe that was when the second chapter of my life began. Consistent with the character and sense of humor God sometimes shows, the name of our street in H.B. was Newman Avenue.

New Man.

Four months after I moved out of the San Fernando Valley, I was awakened from sleep by what felt like someone lifting up my bed and shaking it like a beach towel that's been laying in the sand.

In January of 1994, what would have been the ninth month of my lease, the Northridge Earthquake hit just five miles from my old apartment complex. It leveled not only my former home, but also many others close by. Of course, I went by to check on my manager, who was fine, and to take a look at my old place. I wanted to see what I would have been up against had I still lived there. My old apartment was still vacant, but the bedroom window was boarded up, and so was the entire front entrance of the complex. The entryway, which was one huge glass window, had shattered inward, covering the entire entrance—which was also the main emergency exit for the complex and just a few steps from my front door. The window in my bedroom had also shattered inward, all over the spot left vacant by the absence of my bed. (Turns out, it was a little more difficult renting that room out than my former landlord expected. Good thing ...)

I never heard from the company that owned the complex. I wasn't sure if the cracks in the walls, which they told our remodeling crew to cover up with paint, caulk, and plaster, had anything to do with that—but who knows? The apartments were closed for a long time while they totally rebuilt the place.

ALL PART OF THE PLAN

I had been living in Huntington Beach for about a year and a half when I bumped into Jane, the girl I had hung out with after reading that passage in Jeremiah. She was in town from Fresno, and wanted to talk to me. We met up and had dinner. It felt awkward, because we had a shared past that both of us knew wasn't a healthy one. I can't remember who apologized first, probably because what I do remember sort of took center stage during the conversation.

Jane told me that she allowed me to have my way that day because she remembered what I had told her about the verse, and wanted to see God take everything away from me.

!

The rest of the conversation is obviously private, but suffice it to say that God had been working on her as well. She had since asked Him for forgiveness for what she'd done, and had come to Huntington Beach for the purpose of confessing to me—to which I replied that there wasn't anything to confess.

The point? Sometimes we don't see the purpose, sometimes we do. In this case, it was clear to me that God had intended for me to go through what I did in order to see the truth about myself and the truth about Him. I guess that God really does have a plan, one that goes well beyond just my experience, and that despite everything I might not like about that plan, in the end it's always the best one.

NEW WINE, NEW WINESKINS

I spent about three years away from music and bands, and then I believe God gave me the opportunity to be involved in all of that once more when Stavesacre came along. I really wanted to write songs again, to sing about what I had gone through, but I wasn't sure if it was a good idea. I was hesitant because I didn't want to do what I wanted to do, but what God wanted.

I didn't want to be a part of music the way I had been in the past, I knew that much. I didn't want it to dominate my life and my mind, which I admit is a fight I still struggle with today—the difference being that I know the fight is happening and is necessary. Also, if I was going to sing in a band again, it would be because God simply gave me the ability to do so, and I would glorify Him by using that ability. No more token evangelism. No more preaching at shows to make the Christian kids happy, or to satisfy some utilitarian insecurity of my own. I wanted to leave evangelism, as an aspect of a band, to people who were capable of following up on the lives of those who God had drawn to Him. No more preaching at the show and then driving away, leaving behind the people who might have become Christians. (I know that God takes care of His people just as faithfully as He calls them, but I believe Christians in true ministry are responsible to follow up on the people to whom they are ministering.) I just wanted to be honest, and I hoped it would show in my life—that character would be my witness. I felt that, regarding musicians and entertainers, most of the time, words from some guy on a stage tended to take away from their truth—whenever I heard a band preaching during a show, I would wonder if they were living lives similar to the one I had been living during my time in the Crucified. I wondered if they were preaching because they felt a call from God to do so, or because they just thought that was how things worked. It didn't help much remembering all the times when I heard some kid preaching and I could tell by what he was saying that he was just as lost "preaching" as I had been. I didn't want to be a part of that again.

I wanted the music to be the focus, and I wanted to make the music great. By making music that was powerful in a creative sense, I felt God would be glorified. My initial thought was to speak only when I felt like I was being led to do so. If I was certain that God was putting something on my heart, I would say whatever that was. I was also determined to come to an understanding of what God wanted. Did He want every band to be evangelistic? Did He want music to be considered ministry? The only way to find that out that could really be trusted was to read His Word and objectively search out His will regarding the whole matter.

These days, I don't speak much. I believe that through the years, I've actually learned more about what my calling is—with regards to being a Christian—and I believe that part of the life God has given me is between Him and me. The privacy is needed, trust me. I will say that these days, I see myself as a Christian first, and a musician later. The burdens God has placed on my heart are not wearisome, and that makes me all the more confident that I'm on the right track.

I also don't want to discredit who we are as Christian men of character by using "opportunities" onstage as a platform for my faith. For me ... I don't really see those moments onstage as opportunities. There are people who do, and to them I say, follow your convictions, and I will follow mine. I don't want to hide the Gospel, but I also don't want to use it as a tool to gain fans. And I don't want to use my profession as a tool to gain souls, because I don't believe that's how you truly gain souls. I don't want people to come to my shows and pay to hear the Gospel. (Just like I don't want to hear anyone preaching their beliefs to me when I go to a show or watch a movie.) Why would I force my hand when I was the one with the microphone? I want to be sensitive to and respectful of the trust of others, while holding fast to my faith as the one true faith. I don't want to use a gimmick or trickery to get people to hear the Gospel; I want to rely on the Holy Spirit to guide me and to draw people around me to Him. My prayer is to be a part of the lives of those people who I am around consistently, to find my place—in not only evangelism, or ministry, or work, but also in simple living—in the two greatest commandments: worshiping the Lord God with all my heart, soul, and mind; and loving my neighbor as I love myself.

ELEVEN

he biRTh of Night Town

People are always asking about how God has worked in the band, but I think that most of the time, they have a predetermined idea of what the term "God's work" means, which is too bad. There are valuable lessons in humility, kindness, and simply, love, which often are overlooked in the pursuit of finding out specific details. The question, "How has God worked in the band ...?" can usually be translated to, "How many people have been saved through the band?" Although I do believe that no one is ever saved by us, I do understand why people want to know these things. We are here to do God's work, and part of His work is evangelism, but, as I've stated countless times, I do believe that evangelism is a calling for God's people, and not necessarily bands-that-God's-people-are-in. There is a difference between having an evangelical walk with God and the specific calling of being an evangelist (such as Billy Graham). Plus, and maybe more importantly, there is so much more to God's work than just evangelism. If things like altar call statistics evaluated everything about our faith, as if Christianity were a sport or a business plan, we'd miss out on all the other good stuff. For still more perspective, the following is a story that I wanted to add to illustrate the way God has often worked in my life, through life as a singer in a rock band.

In 1998, before Jeff left and Ryan and Neil joined Stavesacre, the band had the opportunity to go overseas for two weeks to play three festivals, filling the time in-between the festivals with enough club dates to keep us busy. The "tour" was booked around festivals in three places: Gothe, former East) Germany; Alingsos, Sweden; and finally Stockholm, Sweden. The first festival was supposed to be followed by some club dates in Berlin and then northern Germany, where we would find our way up through Sweden by way of Gotesburg, then Alingsos, and on to familiar territory in Stockholm, where we had been two or three times before. While we had dates at the beginning (Germany), middle (Alingsos), and end (Stockholm), we had nothing in between, and were hoping to fill them with ... anything.

The first festival of the tour was "Freakstock." It was put on by some fairly radical German Christians in a small town (Gothe) at a horseracing track out in the middle of nowhere. We were told there would be "lodging"—a dubious term, something we would soon learn the hard way—and meals, and that we would be taken care of regarding transportation to Berlin. What I have just written was all that we knew of the trip, but also knowing that most of the tour was being handled by our English-speaking friends in Sweden, we didn't worry too much about the details. Any excuse to go would have been enough. Hey, we were going to Europe. And they were paying us.

When we arrived in Germany, a young man who was chain-smoking in the waiting area of the airport picked us up. Now, having played in Germany once before at the Christmas Rock Night festival (in a town about forty-five minutes from Düsseldorf, called Ennepetal), we had already been exposed to Christianity from an entirely different perspective than the one we were used to, an experience which in fact helped each of us to stop seeing God as an American with "American Values." We'd met German Christians who said bad words and drank beer, but who were completely devoted to their faith. At first it blew our minds, then when the reality of what we were learning caught up with us, it was just humbling. (Does culture dictate what God sees as sin, or were we just holding people to our ever-changing standards?) We'd been taught a new perspective on our faith, but we'd also only experienced these people for a short time, and were soon back to America and around familiar and typical lifestyles. Coming back to Germany, but this time with the "Jesus Freaks" who put on Freakstock, we were in for a whole new thing ...

The guy spoke very little English. We exchanged some informal greetings and got the basic message across: Let's load up and get to the festival. When our baggage came through, we piled everything in one spot, and so naturally, the guy offered to help us with our gear. Of course, of course. He tucked his cigarette firmly into the corner of his mouth, picked up a couple guitars, and made for the door. As he approached an elevator that would take us to his car, one of the guitars slipped out of his hand and hit the floor with a loud noise that echoed throughout the airport.

"Ah, f---!"

Uhh. Whoa. (teehee) We all looked at each other, shocked and giggling. Meanwhile, he had stepped inside the elevator, then stood staring at us with a blank look on his face. With no real idea what was ahead of us, we followed.

When we arrived at Freakstock, we were introduced to a small festival set up with two main stages in a large field and a couple smaller stages in some of the buildings scattered around the festival grounds. The "Jesus Freaks" were all over the place, guys and girls, mostly punks and guys that looked like Slayer, all casually lounging around the grounds. We hadn't managed much real conversation with the driver on the way to the festival—while he didn't speak much English, we spoke even less German. With some effort, he explained to us that the Jesus Freaks were a community of people mostly from the streets and the German punk scene, who had come to Christ and fallen in with each other as their body of fellowship. We learned that they were very zealous about their faith. They sang songs and made T-shirts proclaiming their Christianity, something that, in a place with the history and culture of Germany, was done at some risk.

There are people over there, not a lot of them, but enough, who really will kill you for being a Christian—this wasn't something they were doing with the intention of fitting in at a youth function or to join a Christian bowling team. He then told us that we had missed the "parade," which was too bad, because they had formed a caravan of about a hundred cars, packed them with people—some riding the rooftops and the hoods—and driven through the surrounding towns singing their songs and waving flags. All to let people know: "Freakstock is coming."

When we were loaded in completely, we were shown to our lodging: green army tents, with six or eight cots in each. Blankets and a pillow. I would love to say that we graciously accepted these humble places to sleep. I would love to say that. But ... it would be a lie. We were pretty freaked out by the "lodging"—the tents had open floors, with grass, frogs, bugs, etc. crawling around; there were no windows, and therefore no ventilation; a community shower—you get the picture. At night, it was so cold that we would dress in full clothing, even wearing some of the sweatshirts we'd brought to sell (because they had hoods), and pile blanket after blanket on top of ourselves. But in the morning, just minutes after the sun came up and hit the dark green tents, the temperature went way up—by the time we forced ourselves out of bed, at like 8 a.m. (not very rock 'n' roll), we were all sprawled out, practically naked, legs and arms hanging over the edges of our cots, sweating like pigs.

The thing is ... it's easy to get spoiled. Touring the Christian Circuit—churches, huge festivals in the States, entertainment budgets—we were used to hotels, dinner and lunch, and backstage "green rooms." We had a little difficulty adjusting to the do-it-yourself, do-the-best-with-what-you-can approach to touring. Sad. It was a difficult realization to me, knowing that we were so accustomed to the amenities of the alternate-reality that is Christian industry touring life. Thankfully, none of us spoke German, and so we couldn't even find the person to gripe to who could have done something about our complaints. We were spared from making ourselves the ungrateful Americans, which, looking back now, I'm sooo very grateful for. With nowhere to whine and no one to whine to, we were going to be sleeping in tents. Or outside. Deal with it.

Things got better. We bumped into some familiar faces: Royal and Selfmindead (sic) of Sweden/Norway were play-ing the festival, and so we immediately grabbed onto them and did not let go. (They didn't seem at all bothered by the tents ...) The people of the festival were really nice and took care to introduce us to some of the folks around the grounds. They helped us get our merchandise booth set up and made sure we had what we needed. When it came time for dinner, we were fed in a line, next to a huge vat of soup, a giant bowl of salad, and a basket of bread. Everyone sat at big tables and ate together, and most everybody seemed to be in a good mood.

I was really enjoying myself. It was like, the general attitude of everyone there made me feel too embarrassed and ungrateful to complain—it took away from the good feeling of meeting people from completely different worlds. I think it rubbed off on us all, and soon we were all fine. (Mostly. Never did dig on the public-shower-nude-German-guy-brushing-his-teeth-right-next-to-me thing ...)

The show was great, the crowd was better. They seemed so happy to have a show to watch in the first place, on top of the fact that German people just love rock music. (Thing is: There was less attitude from the crowds over there than one typically witnesses at a lot of American shows. It was nice to have a break from people too cool to really enjoy themselves ...) We had made friends with some of the other bands by the time we played, including an apparently legendary German band called "the Circumcised," who were playing a farewell show at the festival that year. After we played, they invited us to sit with them in the backstage area, and share stories. Sharing stories. On purpose! What a great thing to do. Unfortunately, over here, we so rarely take time to do that, instead tending to go to what has become the default first conversation—negative things, gripes. But over there, we shared tales from the road, had some laughs, and it was wonderful, easily one of the better experiences I've had touring. I sat across the table from strangers who made me feel comfortable and heard stories about people I'd never met and places I'd never been. They sang songs. We drank German beer, made fun of each other, had fellowship, and never once did I feel the grip of fear or negativity that so often surrounds life over here. (An ironic twist: In a backstage area where beer was free and the drink of choice, I didn't see one person drunk. Would the same be true here? It was strange, but the freedom I felt seemed to heighten my desire for self-control. Why?)

For some perspective on the Jesus Freaks: They had their own band. With outreach being the main thrust of the community, we were told to be sure to catch their crowd pleaser, "Accept Jesus Christ." A sample of the subtle lyrics:

Accept Jesus Christ you m------f---ers!
Accept Jesus Christ you m------f---ers!
Accept Jesus Christ you m------f---ers!

So, they do things a little different over there. (Either that, or someone was playing a joke on the gullible Americans, which would also be pretty funny.)

When it came time to leave for the show in Berlin, we packed our bags into a van and were taken there by a couple of the Jesus Freaks. These two guys spoke less English than the guy from the airport, so we didn't talk much on the trip there. (We wouldn't have been able to carry on a conversation anyway, because we were all too busy tucking our heads between our knees and holding on for dear life ... Jesus Freaks drive fast.)

Pretty soon, we all would've loved to have been able to speak a little German though, because when we got to Berlin, the guys simply dropped us off in front of the club, and left. It dawned on us as we watched them drive away that we had no real idea or plan as to what we were going to do beyond that moment. We had had no contact with the German promoter who was supposed to be handling our shows that week and had no idea where we were staying or how we would get around. We were foreigners in a country on a different continent, and we didn't speak the language.

Oh my.

Looking back now, I think God wanted to drive home the little lesson in humility and appreciation that we

CHAPTER ELEVEN

thought we learned back at Freakstock. I remember praying that God would just watch over us and help us to get
home. Presented with only the option of trusting Him, I
was terrified and thrilled at the same time. It was as if we
were in a spot where God just had to make it work out, and
I remember thinking, "Just watch. Just watch Him take care
of you." Sometimes, the still small voice of the Holy Spirit
shows up in the oddest of places.

We went inside the club, a bar called "Wild at Heart,"
and looked for the owner. Ah! She was in! (Here begins a
long list of events that I'm hoping you will just enter the
"Praise God" for me in the spots where you find it appropriate. Trust me, those words exploded in my mind often
throughout the following weeks. Some other words popped
into my head at other, more terrifying moments; I'll let you
make up your own in those instances.) The owner's name
was Leah, and she spoke English. Breathe.

When we introduced ourselves to Leah, she sort of
opened her mouth in surprise and stepped back, slightly
shocked. She explained her surprise by saying that she
hadn't heard from the promoter in over a month and
figured we weren't coming. She had no idea that we were
in Germany. She also had made no reservations for our
lodging, stopped promoting the show once she decided we
weren't coming, and had no idea where were supposed to
be playing next or how we were going to get there.

Awesome.

Could we get a hotel? "You're in Berlin in the middle of
the summer; there are no hotels."

Oh.

Was there any food or backstage area? "You can put your
gear in the dry storage room by the cooler. I've no budget
for meals, but you can have a case of beer. There's a pizza

parlor across the street."

Already preparing to sleep on the street and busk for change, we nearly put ourselves out of our misery by walking out into traffic when she said, "Okay, everyone relax. I'll have some people spread the word that you're here and will be playing tonight. We'll figure out where you'll sleep when the time comes."

We had no gear, save for our guitars, amps, drumsticks and cymbals.

"You can probably borrow from the band that is playing tonight. No problem."

Okay ... oh by the way, who was playing?

"A great band—they're called Nuclear Tribunal. Death metal, really fast. They'll be here soon; I'll introduce you to them."

Here, it gets good.

We went across the street to the pizza parlor Leah mentioned. Morale was not high. We were about to play a show to an empty bar in a country we were unfamiliar with and uncomfortable in, and we weren't sure where we were going to sleep or where we were going next. We were hot and irritable ... and hungry.

Without naming names, one member of Stavesacre wasn't handling the situation too well, and it had begun to show. At the pizza place, everyone had ordered but him, and we were sitting at a table waiting for our food. Ordering food in Germany and not speaking German is not an easy thing ("it's like they have a different word for everything!"), but three of us had managed it. We'd heard just enough random trivia to know that "pepperoni" over there is not a spicy salami-like meat, but actually peppers. If you order "pepperoni pizza" in Europe, you are most likely going to end up with a green pizza that tastes bad. This information was just enough to make a person nervous to order anything, but if you're patient and polite, you can get the job done. This particular member of the band was in no mood for patience or politeness, and before we realized what was happening, he was yelling at the poor little Italian-German guy behind the counter. Aware of the problem just long enough to look over at him, he turned to us and yelled out, "WHAT AM I SUPPOSED TO DO? THIS GUY DOESN'T SPEAK ANY ENGLISH!"

No witty response could match the statement, "We're in Germany, remember?" With our best apologetic body language—and a concerned eye—we looked over to the guys behind the counter. They were shaking their heads and saying words that even the worst German student learned in one week of class, but eventually they made him a cheese pizza, and we all got to sit down and focus.

With frustration showing its ugly head in the form of bad attitudes and hot tempers, the pizza parlor incident served the function of shaking us up from our grim outlook and forcing us to turn our eyes off our circumstances and back on the Lord. This was pivotal, and with some food in the stomach, it was easier to think clearly. I had been pretty shaken up by the ride over (lots of zigging and zagging, lots of slamming brakes and lead feet), but I was feeling better. After our meal and a little prayer, we all felt better and were able to see the situation for what it was: an adventure. The reality was that we were powerless and lost, and we had no one to depend on but God. (Somehow this seemed to be a "new" revelation, but you know how that goes.) The more I thought about it, the more I realized that we were always in this situation, we just rarely experienced it with such drastic circumstances. We prayed about our predicament and realized these things together, and—maybe because we had no other choice—we tried to relax and enjoy ourselves.

We went back across the street to meet the other band.

Nuclear Tribunal arrived at the club a few hours before the show. The band was made up of three Russian guys with prison tattoos and long hair, who spoke exactly zero English, and one half-Persian, half-German guy with long curly hair named Raoul. Raoul was the singer; he had no prison tattoos, but was sporting black leather pants with laces up the outer seams and big boots. It turned out that Raoul did speak English. Fluent English.

This was displayed wonderfully when, as his band began to play their set, he ran out through the front door of the empty club to scream to us and the few people sitting outside, "WE ARE NUCLEAR TRIBUNAL, AND NOW I WILL SHOVE MY FIST UP YOUR F------ A----!"

We all took that as a hint, and went inside to watch them play. If you were curious about their sound, let's just say the name says it all. By the time we took the stage, there were actually some people there. Slightly high from the adventure we found ourselves in, we had a blast. Halfway through the set, the club was full. Apparently when Leah says she will get the word out around town that a show is happening, she really means it, and people actually come. The room was small, but the place was packed, and the people were into the music. By the time we finished, we felt ten feet tall, even though each of us knew we still had to figure out where to sleep that night—not to mention, that week. We couldn't let the fear of our situation get in the way of the fact that we had just played a club in Berlin and did well. We met some of the locals and made a few acquaintances. It was an awesome feeling. Leah came backstage with a tray full of drinks "on the house" and a smile on her face.

"You boys did so well!" Celebrating all around.

"I have found you a place to sleep, too!" More celebrating.

Where? we asked.

Through the backstage door ... in walks Raoul, leather

pants and all.

"You've all met Raoul, right?"

———————————————❋———————————————

Raoul lived just down the street, in a two-bedroom flat. We all walked down to his place, preparing for whatever kind of house the fist-shoving singer of Nuclear Tribunal might live in. The apartment wasn't too bad: no scarier than any bachelor pad I've ever lived in. No blood-drenched walls or coffins in the corner. No heroin needles stuck in the ceiling. Just a two-bedroom apartment, Berlin-style. (The weirdest thing about the place was the bathroom: The toilet was in the smallest room imaginable, with barely enough room for one to stand inside and close the door. The shower was actually in the kitchen, and you had to use a small stepladder to get into it, as the bottom of the shower was attached to, and level with, the sink. Sort of an exhibitionist's dream shower.)

The person who lived there didn't match the person we had met earlier; in fact, his whole demeanor changed once we got to his house. Raoul was a film student who loved music and movies … and, as we eventually found out, fishing. (More about that later …) After talking for a few minutes, he told us how to work the shower, and then, as if to help us sleep, explained to us that our next show was in a town not too far away (we knew the name of the place we were playing, and he was familiar with it) and that he would help us to get to the train and set us on the right route. He then showed us all to different places to sleep and went to his room and closed the door. Jeff and I shared the other bedroom; Dirk and Sam slept in the living room.

The next morning, as I made my way to the shower, I entered the kitchen and stopped dead in the middle of the room. Spread out on the table was a huge feast. There were fresh baked rolls; about ten or fifteen different jams and spreads for the rolls, fresh juice, milk, and coffee. Raoul had been up for a while and had gone down to the corner bakery, then spent his own money taking care of guests he had only found out he would be entertaining the night before. He'd even set out clean towels and soap.

After my shower, I went in to the living room, where Dirk and Sam were already up and talking to Raoul. At some point, he'd gathered all the information we needed for our trip to northern Germany and the next show. He let us know what train we were going to use and offered to take us himself. (We had met a guy at the show the night before who was familiar with American hardcore bands and managed a bit of conversation with him as well. He told us at the show that if we needed any help getting around the next day, he would be happy to help. I took this with the usual grain of salt that such promises usually warrant, but of course, he showed up! What? Oh, you really meant what you said? Hey, easy, I'm from America, we aren't used to that sort of thing ...)

While Raoul said he was happy to help, it seemed like a surprise to him that we were so shocked at his generosity. Besides, he was more interested in something else: music. He was sharing all the music he loved with us, playing different bands for us, telling their stories. (This was the first time we had heard of the new wave of dirty Scandinavian/ European rock bands, with groups like the Backyard Babies, Gluecifer, Turbo Negro, and the Hellacopters. They were all like the mean-spirited and ugly big brothers of bands like the Hives.) He had vinyl, posters of shows, and a million different bits of information. With every minute that passed, the image of the guy we had met the night before seemed more and more laughable. We were actually nervous about sleeping at this guy's house?

When we finally had to go, Dirk and I rode with Raoul; Sam and Jeff rode with the hardcore guy. On the way to the train station, Raoul asked us about our faith and our lives. He told us that he wasn't a Christian, but he believed in God and knew that He existed. We of course asked why, and then he told us this story, which I will now attempt to retell:

Before the Berlin wall came down, Raoul lived in a small town in East Germany. When the wall was still up, he used to fish every chance he got at a quiet little lake near his home. When it came down, his fishing hole was ruined by the development that took over many parts of what had been undeveloped land. A freeway went up right by his fishing spot. The building of the freeway, and eventually the cars that would constantly pass by, soon spoiled the peaceful afternoons he spent there.

There was a lake in India that was rumored to have the biggest freshwater fish in the world, and so, in search of some peaceful and rewarding fishing, Raoul packed his things and made the trip. Once there, he took a train and then a bus to the little town that was closest to the lake. Once in the town, the lake was still a five-day hike through a jungle, so he set off alone in search of it.

About three days into his hike, there was a storm. Raoul woke to a loud rushing sound, like an airplane landing. He had been sleeping in his hammock, which he had hung high up in a tree to keep him safe from wild animals. The trees shook, and he could sense a lot of movement on the ground below him, but in the dark, there wasn't much he could do but return to sleep. The next morning, he woke to find that a huge mudslide had passed through the jungle below, flooding the surrounding area with mud and sweeping away all of the gear, including his pole and compass, which he had fastened to the tree beneath him. He was stuck in the middle of the jungle with little food and no way to get back to civilization. Since attempting to find the lake was a waste with no fishing gear or pole, he began hiking back through the mud and rain, soon realizing that he did not have enough food to get back. The journey was taking too long, and he was covered in mud and soaked to the bone.

He said that at one point, while knee-deep in mud, he cried out to God and asked Him to save him. He said that there was just no way he could make it back, and he knew it, but somehow he thought God might help him.

Miraculously, he found his bearings, even in the storm, and staggered back to the little town. One of the people in town gave him the money to get back home, and from then on, he swore that God had saved him, and that even if he did not claim to be a Christian, it wasn't because he didn't believe in God.

Now while this story has no typical Christian ending, where Raoul goes on to tell us that he is now a pastor or something, I believe that it was a wonderful opportunity for us to share our faith with another person in a way that fit in with God's larger, more life-changing will. He was clearly happy to share it with us, and I think he was appreciative of the fact that we actually listened to him. Though we weren't able to lead him to salvation, or whatever it is that we do, I would not be surprised to find that Raoul was now a Christian. (Of course, knowing how people tend to let things fade, I would be equally un-surprised to find that Raoul was now tormented daily by what he knows is a denial of the truth on his part.) I really couldn't tell you, but I believe that God used us, in some way, to further His will in Raoul's life. Whenever I have doubts about the route that we have chosen with the band, I think about opportunities like the one with Raoul, I'm reminded of that day, and I

CHAPTER ELEVEN

find a little comfort. I know that for some time on earth, I was part of His will. Did our presence there produce results that a person could measure? Probably not, at least not then, but our lives aren't measured by human beings. Somehow, some way, God will use that divine conversation in Raoul's life. Amazing. We didn't have any idea who this person was just the day before, and had we not been willing to play a show in a club like Wild At Heart, or to stay at the home of a guy like Raoul, we would never have had the opportunity at all.

Raoul saw us to the train; he even waited there at the station while we left. I think he was sad to see us go, but we were probably sadder. We were back out on the road again, alone in Germany. Right around this point, we realized just how much we valued luxuries like "Vanna" and a trailer. We had all our baggage and the gear we had brought for the tour, but nowhere to put it, and comically ... no way to get it from one point to another. We formed a sort of "daisy-chain" everywhere we went: One person as far ahead as we were willing or needed to go would stand guard, while each of the rest of us ran back and forth from the point the gear and bags had previously been, dropping them off at his feet. Imagine yourself driving two cars at a time, getting out every fifty yards or so, running back to the other car, passing the first, going fifty yards, getting out ... and so on. We must have looked pretty funny to the people at the train stations, the bus stops, and the airports. "Oh look, how cute! A little team of leapfrogging Americans!"

We headed up to a town called Rostock, on the northern coast of Germany, at a port close to Sweden. It was only Tuesday, and we needed to find a place to go after Germany. Sam got in contact with some people he had met back at Cornerstone one year, who were in missionary training in the town of Copenhagen, Denmark. They invited us to come and stay with them for the four days we needed to kill. Saved! We would leave Germany, land in Sweden, and then take a ferry from the same port over to Copenhagen. So we had that covered, but as for the show ...

In Rostock, we were supposed to play a club/art gallery that was on a converted naval ship. The boat was crazy, three levels of everything from performance art to a club with a deejay spinning music. Of course, when we got there, they had no idea who we were or that we had any intentions of playing a show. Too bad ... probably would have been a lot of fun. They showed us the way out, and we ended up standing on the street with all our gear and bags, with no idea where to go next.

Feeling energized from our encounter with Raoul, we realized that we were still being a huge bunch of sissies, so we decided to force ourselves to have a good time with the uncertain circumstances. We stayed in Rostock that night—finding a hotel there was much easier to do than in Berlin. The city of Rostock was holding some sort of outdoor festival, so we all showered up and went out to sample German nightlife. There were vendors with beer and food, rides, and a giant sound system at the center of a small carnival on the boardwalk. We walked around, people-watching and joking with each other; it was a great time. I remember watching all of these young adults and middle-aged German people get their boogie on, all of them singing and dancing around the sound system that was apparently being guest-hosted by some popular deejay/radio personality. I don't know, maybe I was a little emotional from all the surrounding circumstances, but I remember feeling a little jealous: I have never seen anything that at least appeared to be as unpretentious as this in America. (I just can't see something like that happening without people being totally uptight or too concerned with how they look to anyone who might be watching. I also can't see something like this happening here in the States without loads of people getting completely smashed. Drunk and belligerent, fighting. Rioting. It seems like most of the time I go out while on the road in the States, the night ends up with someone—or many someones—throwing up, starting fights, going to jail, or just generally doing things they will regret the next day. Any state, any city. Was there a class I missed or something? Is this normal? Don't get me wrong—I'm sure there are drunk people and date rapes in other places than America. I just feel like there is a definite difference in the way people approach "hanging out" over here as opposed to the other places I've been. It's hard to explain, but I see it like this: In Europe, it seemed to be more embarrassing for people to lose all control—like a decision rather than an expectation; while in the states, it seems to be less of question of whether or not, but more like, "Who first?")

After hangin' with the good people of Rostock until the small hours, we went back to our little hotel and slept in real beds for the first time in what seemed like a week. The next day, we crossed over to Sweden.

Right around this time, we were all reading a lot while on the road, and we happened to be passing around two books: *U2 at the End of the World*, by Bill Flanagan; and *Addicted to Mediocrity*, by Franky Schaeffer. We had heard about *Addicted* from our friend Bill Power and the MxPx guys, who had been telling us about the book for a while. A friend, Wayne Everett, who at the time was playing drums for Starflyer 59, had mentioned the U2 book to us a few times as well, commenting that some of the looks into the spirituality of the band were pretty refreshing. Both books were rumored to echo a lot of the same things that we were feeling at the time, so we gave them a spin.

I had just finished *Addicted* when we got to Sweden, and so I started in on *End of the World* once we got to the ferry that would take us into Copenhagen. It just so happened that at that same time, I was "rediscovering" U2's follow-up to *Achtung, Baby*, the album, *POP*. As you probably know, this was an album that, compared with some of their other efforts, didn't do so well. (You know, sold a measly 5 million copies or something ...) But as a Christian, rediscovering that album changed my life, and listening to it while reading *End of the World* was the perfect accompaniment to that trip. The sound of the album was the sound of Europe at the time; you could hear it everywhere we went. The sound of the album felt like my very own soundtrack to the tour, but the lyrics were what hooked me completely. I had just begun questioning the contemporary version of Christianity that I had grown so weary of, and to hear of people, Bono in particular, going through times of doubt and question somehow comforted me. There's a lot of honesty on that album, more than some people were probably ready to hear. Anyone expecting to hear a more evangelical U2 (maybe due to the success of *Achtung, Baby*) was sadly disappointed to hear a guy going through times of doubt and anger, but I wasn't disappointed at all. I never worshiped the ground Bono walked on, but I did feel that some of the things he had to say resonated with me, and knowing there was anyone else out in the world who was willing to ask the hard questions of his faith was definitely a comforting thought.

Here was this guy who had had so many more experiences, and with a far greater influence than myself, with awkward and seemingly contradicting spiritual incidents, and he was just throwing it all out there, letting the world in on some of his struggles. It was liberating. Then, reading the book, and knowing the way people lumped so many judgments on that band, just confirmed my belief that perception really isn't everything. There were things going on in their songs and in their lives that seemed to contradict a lot that so many people had believed to be true. But the things that were going on were only contradicting to people who were ready to believe the worst, and who couldn't possibly know the people they were talking about. People were making so many judgments, based on speculation about U2's perceived lack of "good deeds" and the subject matter of their newer songs. Reading the real story about them, for me, wasn't so much a comforting experience—in terms of asking, "How are these guys doing spiritually?"—as it was a little encouragement that where I was headed in my approach to the public perception of my spiritual life was the right direction.

I also loved that Bono and the other Christians of the band didn't just hole up in their tour busses or hotels. They lived, they had experiences, and they took chances. Couldn't—or rather, wouldn't—a Christian be more effective in that sort of environment? Instead of hiding in churches, going to Christian schools, Christian hair salons, eating Christian breakfast cereal, etc., wouldn't we be more effective as lights in dark places? This was probably the point where Stavesacre's desire to break out of the so-called "Christian Market" turned a corner. Not only did we believe that there was something decidedly "ungodly" about it, we now started to see that there was opportunity to be of use as Christian men, by being in the places where Christian men and women didn't normally make themselves available. Let the critics say what they want. They can accuse us of having "fellowship with darkness" due to the company we keep (rather than an accurate appraisal of our spiritual lives), while we can have clear consciences knowing that we aren't hiding our lamps under peck measures. (Most of the band, including Ryan once he joined, have read that book. We took a term from it that showed up later on our split EP with Denison Marrs and on our self-titled album, *(stavz-a-ker)*. "Night Town" was, in a way, our celebration of the new way we wanted to approach our lifestyle and our faith. Meaning, live.)

Anyways …

When we got to Copenhagen, Sam's friend, Jon Eric, met us at the ferry station. He took us to the mission house that he and his fellow Youth With A Mission brothers and sisters were sharing. Y.W.A.M. (usually pronounced, "wai-wam") is a missionary training program for young people, and Jon Eric and his roommates were part of the outreach group for the city of Copenhagen, in Denmark. I was surprised to find Christian men and women sharing the same house—a major taboo to most of the Christian people I had grown up around—but after a short time, I stopped thinking about it. I was too blown away by their love for each other and their care for us to be thinking about taboos and token boundaries. They took us in and fed us, giving us beds and showers. They cooked a meal together, each person with his or her own duty, and then we all sat around the dinner table that first night and got to know each other. It's funny, once you stop looking for the worst everywhere you go, you tend to notice the good things that people are actually doing. These people were just Christians in training to be missionaries for the Gospel. That's it. They displayed their desire by taking care of us, and it was inspiring.

We spent those four days with them, walking all around Copenhagen. We were taken to a place in the middle of the city called "Christiania," where there were a lot of shows and young people, and where the group felt a desire to be a help and ministering presence. Christiania attempted to secede from Copenhagen in the '60s, and to start its own city (maybe even country …) within the city limits. There was one major reason for this:

Christiania is marijuana heaven. (I'm sure that back then,

there were all sorts of other reasons they sought secession, but as far as right now is concerned, it seems to be all about the weed.) Their desire, as I understood it, was to create a safe and independent community of peaceful living. Marijuana was a major part of the culture of the people of this community, and they wanted to have their own laws regarding it. They also championed the cause of stamping out the "hard drugs"—heroin in particular—that were claiming the lives of so many residents of the city of Copenhagen. They didn't succeed in their attempt at establishing a completely independent country, but somehow they were allowed to continue on with their cause. Now they are a "commune" of sorts, with their own laws, their own economy (built around the best handmade bicycles on earth, "the Christiania Bikes"), and their own national pastime: Smoking the weed.

We went walking through "town." Jon Eric showed us where they put on most of their shows, the town park, the town square, and a little place called the "hash market"— which prohibited cameras and hard drugs, but allowed huge guards armed with pit bulls and merchants who sold bricks of hash the size of soap bars. (I saw one guy rolling a joint that was literally ten feet long ... don't ask me. Besides, that was nothing compared to the pot plants that were bigger than the trees in my frontyard.) There were people sleeping everywhere.

Jon said that the sad part of it all was that, despite all the talk of "no hard drugs," many people there were using them. Some people used Christiania as a place to go while they were getting clean, but while there were many people there who were just part of the culture, there were a lot of people in bondage, dependent on one vice or another. While we walked around, Jon Eric and his friends said hello to a few people, made themselves approachable, and mostly just made themselves comfortable. I liked their reasoning:

Many of these people were very guarded, and they wanted them to see that they weren't there to take from them or rule their lives, but to be available and kind, and in turn, little by little, the people seemed to respond.

I also got the impression that Jon Eric and his friends not only cared about these people, but that they were even a little protective of the relationships they had worked so hard to build there, and that ultimately they would trust God to provide the opportunity for His Gospel to go forward. Again, this theme of living life outside the gates of the Christian community presented itself, only this time I could see it at work.

Each day, we ate lunch outside next to the channels and docks that ran all through their area in Copenhagen. We walked up and down "the Walking Street." We had drinks with our new friends and talked about things that mattered. Less about music and the business of entertainment, more about life, God, faith, and all those things between. It was wonderful, and yet another incredible turn of events in the face of a situation that at one point had been shrouded in uncertainty and full of fear.

In America, I just can't imagine this happening. Surely some church elder or some uptight parent would come undone the moment the word "hash" came into the conversation. Thankfully, in some places, the process of ministry has the chance to take root, grow, and produce actual fruit that is useful to the world we are in.

We stayed there for four days, and not once did one of them ever give us the impression that we weren't welcome. These people, who would probably be cross-examined and rebuked by the Church at home in the States, ministered to us in the most basic and essential ways. I believe that their presence, mixed with the other experiences I mentioned, have been major influences in my life and in shaping Stavesacre to be the band we are now.

CHAPTER ELEVEN

(The saddest thing about this story is that I'm sure there is someone reading it that will be completely freaked out until they know whether or not our good friends there actually smoke out while they're in Christiania. "Forget the great illustration of God's love, we wanna know if any of those kids are smoking pot!" Are you one of those people? Well, for their sakes, not yours, I'll answer that ridiculous question, even though it just kills me to feel like I need to even acknowledge you: no.)

When we left Copenhagen and headed back to familiar Sweden, we were, for the most part, relieved to be back on familiar ground. I was happy to be back in a place that wasn't a total mystery to me, but I was also a little sad that the truly adventurous part of the tour was over. There was something about being completely in the hands of God that gave me so much satisfaction. The rest of the tour went with little difficulty or adventure, although I will say that there are very few places on earth that I would dare to compare with the beauty of Sweden. We watched one of the last shows of the great Royal at the Park Fest in Alingsos, and met some pretty great people. We stayed out late, saw all that we could, and learned a lot about life outside of our comfort zone. I guess the purpose in sharing this was to show that Stavesacre's change in approach to faith and music, and the relationship between the two, came not from sitting around the backstage of some Christian show at a fancy church complaining about inconveniences, but out of living life and allowing for new experiences and perspectives to introduce themselves to us.

SIMPLICITY
A BRIGHT SPOT ALONG THE WAY

While on tour with the Supertones—a horrible tour for a band like Stavesacre—I had a prayer answered.

At this time, the Supertones were absolutely huge and could do just about whatever they wanted to do, including bringing a rock band like Ghoti Hook and an aggressive rock band like us on tour as opening acts. It was a cool gesture on their part, and maybe a wise decision on paper (more styles of music, more kids), but in the long run, it was a seven-week tour that felt like it took seven months.

Stavesacre and Ghoti Hook (also know as "The Hookers") became close on that tour for many reasons—we enjoyed their company, we liked their music and the show they put on, etc., but we also became close by sharing the same fault: We were both "Not Christian Enough." On that tour, the crowd actually booed us—twice—and we had kids asking us questions like, "You guys are Christians? Where's your horn section?" It was sort of a drag, but we felt we had to do it because it was a chance to play in front of a whole lot of people who had never heard of us before. The Supertones were totally supportive the whole time, which was encouraging, so in the end, it was worth it.

We had some great times with the Supertones and Ghoti Hook and with the crew on the tour, but it was also a trial. Not going over well, night after night, was disheartening. We were constantly faced with the contrast between what we were doing crowd-wise and with merchandise sales, against what a band like the Supertones was doing. It's hard to feel like you're going the right way—even though we all knew that we were playing to a crowd that, for the most part, had no interest in our music. When you see what someone else is doing against what you've been doing, reality is there, plain as day. The thought is: They are making progress; we are spinning our wheels.

I was in the back of the van on our way to a show just outside of Chicago, praying about the tour, the band, and life in general. I asked God if this really was what He wanted me to do with my life. It was just one of those stretches where I felt like I was wasting my time. I asked God if He could maybe let me know whether or not I was where I was supposed to be. I didn't want writing in the sky, just a little clue or something.

We played our first set, and then the Supertones went on. (The show sold out so quickly that we ended up playing twice in the same day, just to let everyone in town have the opportunity to see the bands.) While the 'Tones were on-stage, I walked through the lobby at the front of the venue and headed to the "green room" for dinner.

On my way, a young girl stopped me and asked if I could talk to her for just a second, and I hesitantly said yes. She was sort of shaking, and her lips were trembling. I wasn't sure at first if I should stop, but then I noticed she wasn't nervous, she was crying. I asked her what was wrong. She dismissed my question, introduced herself, and told me what was on her mind. I'll do my best to recall everything she said:

She and her best friend were big Stavesacre fans. They used to listen to our music and wonder about the stories that went on behind the songs. She also told me they were both writing journals to their future husbands, and that they had written in those journals about some of the conversations they had regarding our songs. Then she really started to cry. She said her friend had been coming home from Bible study a few weeks earlier and had been in a car accident. Her friend passed away, and because they were so close, she was given her friend's journal. She wanted me to know how much our music had meant to them, and so she promised herself that she would let me know when we came to town.

She thought I would like to know some of what her friend had written about us, and so she handed me three pieces of paper. Her friend had written a poem that she thought I might like and some thoughts about a few of the songs. She copied them down and gave them to me.

By the time she finished, I was completely overwhelmed. I know that God answers prayer, but to have Him answer so quickly was incredible. This young girl had memorized the poem as best as she could and had written it down on flyers from the show, along with some of the thoughts her friend had written out—just so I would know how much of an effect our music had on her.

I could see how much it meant to her to have the opportunity to tell me everything. The gesture was humbling, and beautiful. This, to me, is ministry.

FINALLY

Out of respect for time, and your patience, I think I need to wrap this up. I never really intended to get this deep into the details, if you can believe that. Stranger still is the fact that I feel like I haven't even scratched the surface.

I really just want you to understand.

I wanted to bring some light to one of the dark corners of our little world, and at this point, I can only hope that I've at least started the process.

I don't know if much has been solved really... except to prove that I have a lot to learn. I think that might be half the reason for this book: to show you and everyone else that I don't know much at all! I am not qualified to lead anyone. I don't feel that calling; I don't feel the convictions that someone who has missed his calling should be feeling. I'm just a Christian guy in a band. Do you realize how many of my friends who play music, or entertain, or are just visible people for one reason or another, feel this way?

Many.

I would even say ... most.

FINALLY

Do we feel God uses us? Yes. Do we feel that He uses us more than the average person? Maybe—depends on whether you're asking about quantity or quality.

I believe that when God calls someone to ministry, they need little in the way of "qualifications." Qualified as defined by whom? He enables them, and that's that. Sure, people learn, they gain experience, they gain wisdom. I would much rather have a pastor who has both studied the Bible inside and out and lived life. (If your soul is as important to you as your body, don't you think you'd like your pastor to be as full of knowledge as your doctor?) But a person can't truly gain that wisdom without God first calling them to do so.

Our nature as fallen beings is to desire what pleases our fallen selves, and we are driven by those desires until God gives us new ones. Then, while coming of age as His children, we learn our place in His plan. It's not that I don't desire to gain wisdom, love, and experience, I do. I simply don't feel called to be a preacher—and I hate feeling obligated to prove that to every other person I bump into at a show. But I also don't want to be a closed door, so I've tried to share some of my feelings and experiences here. I still don't feel called to be a teacher or an evangelist, at least not the kind that many Christians would recognize. I don't feel that pulling me, or leading me, as an actual calling on my life, and certainly not one that I could build some sort of organized ministry around.

In all of the lists of callings that God puts on His people, neither musician nor entertainer is among them. For now, I desire to serve God and humbly reflect who He is with my life. Whatever my purpose as a musician may be, it's no more distinguished than that which I maintained as a waiter or as a coffee shop employee. Through God, I have been used on a large scale through music, but I still feel closer to the smaller ways God has used me. When God gives me the opportunity for evangelism in my personal interaction with people, I consider myself blessed—but I don't feel like I should have to justify myself to some fan just so they won't go around telling people I don't love Jesus anymore. Here, I've opened the door to my personal life to you, and now, maybe, after reading this, you'll think more than twice about judging a brother or sister who hasn't done things exactly as you would have.

Does that set your mind at ease? Knowing that I'm "all right" and that I "check out" with all of your standards or expectations? To be honest, I hope it doesn't. I hope you don't have any special standards or expectations of me, or anyone in a situation similar to mine. Entertainment is not a spiritual gift. If you think it is ... I would argue that you think that only because you are trying to define a spiritual role using worldly wisdom. I would argue that you only think that because some person told you that you should. Where else could it have come from? Not the Bible ...

"Well, just think of how much good for the kingdom he/she could do ..." Every time I hear that reasoning behind this whole mess, I am reminded of why Israel chose Saul over David.

Have you ever said something like, "I just need to know they're right on, and that they talk about Jesus!" Well, doesn't that beg the question: What does "right on" mean? And further, what exactly do you mean when you say, "talk about Jesus"? And what in the world are you so worried about? How can you really know what any musician is ever talking about unless you're in that person's head, knowing their thoughts from beginning to end? You're dealing with artists here, and if you're looking for absolutes in art—or finding them—I might go out on a limb and say ... bad art. Been done before. If you want angels and word-for-word biblical stories for art, please, visit the Sistine Chapel. It's a masterpiece, but it already exists, and now we're trying something new. I'm not being sarcastic, I'm just trying to define our present situation so we can have some clear dialogue.

I would love to see less judgmental attitudes on all levels.

FINALLY

I used to be that kid who counted how many times a band would mention Jesus or God in interviews. I used to doubt the spiritual well-being of strangers, based solely on the lyrical content of their new album. It's not like this is an easy pattern to break out of either, because typically, we want to believe what we've been taught is true. I must admit that in some ways, I still have a problem with this detached stone-throwing—I just direct my stones to a different crowd. I think we need to be a little more gentle and believe the best of our brothers and sisters. "Slow to speak, slow to wrath, but quick to listen" (James 1:19). The Bible says that teachers will be under stricter judgment (James 3:1)—I wonder who will be delivering the stricter judgment? You or I? Don't we know better, as people humbled before God, than to judge one another? Okay, enough ... I'll open this thing back up and never finish it. The story of Stavesacre is not ready to be told, because it's still developing. Please, just remember that there are real people who are truly affected by the things that are said about them. I wrote this to explain how I got here, to answer the questions I asked myself not too long ago: Why do I think this way? Why do I feel this way?

Well, I hope that at least we know a little more. Hopefully by my story, a person might think before they speak or pause before they hurt. If that ever ends up being the case, I will call this long rambling conversation a success.

Thanks.